Craquelins

CRAQUELIN – *A kind of biscuit that crunches between the teeth*

– DICTIONNAIRE FRANÇAIS ILLUSTRÉ ET ENCYCLOPÉDIE UNIVERSELLE, PARIS, 1864

THIS OLD FRENCH WORD is our passport for a baking adventure, as we embark on a tasty world tour of crunchy thin 'craquelin' crackers and cookies. They're quite simply delicious, and in this collection, vegetarian and even vegan-friendly.

Here you will find more than 80 easy-to-prepare recipes and variations. Inspired by ingredients that come to us from the four corners of the globe, craquelins are just the ticket for nibbles or an after-meal treat.

So all aboard! En route! New horizons and flavours beckon... to us the pleasure of discovering them together!

Craquelins

A cookbook of savoury & sweet recipes
for wafer-thin crackers & cookies

Peter Gillies

Illustrations by Magdalena Adomeit

artists·bistro·café·

artists·bistro·café·

enjoy life & love others
be you & have fun

For information about the translations of this book into other languages, please visit our website

www.artistsbistrocafe.com

artists·bistro·café·
is an imprint of
A·B·C· EDITIONS ✦ FRANCE

a small, independent publisher of creative books from off the beaten path, we warmly thank you for your interest and support

Craquelins
A cookbook of savoury and sweet recipes for wafer-thin crackers and cookies

ISBN 978-2-9570286-3-4

✦ ✦ ✦ ✦ ✦ ✦ ✦ ✦

Plaisirs vrais et peu chers !
la joie était complète
Lorsque d'un craquelin
on nous faisait l'emplette

- Amédée Pommier

To my mother…

who first taught me how to bake

*and for whom, more than just a delicious treat,
oven-fresh cakes and cookies have always been
an expression of love*

Where?

Introduction 1

To begin with...

→ Q's & A's 2

The SAVOURY *craquelins*

1. Herbes de Provence 10
2. Wholewheat 12
3. Cracked pepper 14
4. Tomato ~ Black olive 16
5. Worcestershire 18
6. Malted yeast 20
7. Savoury shortcrust 22
8. Sesame 24
9. Garlic ~ Sesame 26
10. Chickpea 28
11. Chili 30
12. Curry ~ Sesame 32
13. Gomashio 34
14. Sambar 36
15. Seaweed 38
16. Coconut ~ Curry 40

The SWEET *craquelins*

1. Hazelnut 44
2. Coffee 46
3. Rolled oats 48
4. Shortbread 50
5. Coconut 52
6. Chocolate 54
7. Chocolate ~ Mint 56
8. Chocolate ~ Orange 58
9. Chocolate ~ Intensely so 60
10. "Ginger nut" 62
11. "Speculaas" 64
12. "Chocolate chip" 66
13. "Digestive biscuit" 68
14. Sugar ~ plain & simple 70
15. Lemon 72
16. Aniseed 74
17. Cinnamon 76
18. Orange 78
19. Pistachio 80
20. Peanut butter 82
21. Wasabi 84
22. Candied ginger 86
23. Sesame 88
24. Matcha 90
25. Tamarind 92
26. Rose water 94
27. Vanilla 96

... and finally

→ A word about... 100

→ Nutritional information 104

A complete list of the recipes and the variations 105

→ Index 108

Introduction

'Wow, these are delicious! And the recipe? It's something you dreamed up? I hope you'll share it with me... '

One fine day, inspired by a chance thought, I set about concocting a new treat for myself, a treat that would be both vegetarian and easy to make. So began my adventure with *craquelins* – an old French word I freely repurpose to mean 'a savoury biscuit or sweet cookie that is both very thin and crunchy.' Soon, my friends and family were enjoying craquelins, too... and pestering me for the recipes! That, as you can probably guess, led to writing this book.

I've collected here the best of my recipes, both savoury and sweet. Some take their cue from wholegrain flours, rolled oats or nuts. Others are ambassadors for more exotic ingredients, such as tamarind, seaweed and wasabi. There are craquelins that put the spotlight on a single distinctive flavour – black pepper, lemon, coconut – and still others that aim to indulge our timeless hankering for favourites like chocolate, vanilla and ginger.

Craquelins are for everyone. They're health-conscious, based on all-natural ingredients and even vegan-friendly. Better still, the doughs typically take just minutes to prepare, so baking a batch or two is a cinch. Savoury craquelins go well with dips and make tasty appetizers on their own, while sweet craquelins are great for snacks, for pairing up with a cup of tea or coffee, or for rounding off a meal as a light dessert.

So here's to craquelins! May they bring you the best of tasty baking pleasures, and most especially, ones you'll enjoy sharing with your friends and family.

Q's & A's

The recipes in this book are straightforward and easily prepared. Even so, the following questions merit the detour, and are worth exploring...

What are the golden rules for the dough?

The dough should be smooth and supple. Not too soft – it shouldn't readily stick to your hand. Not too dry – it shouldn't crack into bits when you roll it out. If the dough is too dry, add more liquid a teaspoon at a time; if the dough is too soft, add a bit more flour.

The use of baking powder as a leavening agent means that craquelin doughs can be baked as soon as they have been mixed. They can also be set aside for a half hour or so without being unduly affected; indeed, a 10 to 15 minute rest tends to render the dough easier to roll out.

The recipes that call for cocoa are calculated to be a bit softer when mixed; cocoa powder is quite dry, and it rapidly absorbs the liquid. If the dough feels too soft at first, leave it to rest for about 10 minutes.

Do they have to be vegan? Or can I use dairy milk and butter?

All of the recipes in this book are vegan-friendly – that is, they use no animal-sourced ingredients. But you can freely adapt the recipes to your own tastes and preferences. Grated or crumbled dairy cheeses can be added as a savoury topping; almond butter and vegan milk can be replaced, gram for gram, by sweet cream butter and dairy milk; and honey can be used for icings.

Which kitchen utensils will I need?

A bowl. A mixing spoon. Occasionally, a mortar and pestle. Now and then, a grater. A rolling pin is essential. Something to sift flour with. A bowl scraper can come in handy at times. So too a wheel-bladed pizza cutter.

Baking paper, preferably unbleached, is virtually indispensable. It allows you to easily transfer the rolled-out dough, sliding it off your work surface or table onto your baking sheet and vice versa when needed.

A proper set of measuring spoons in either metric or imperial gradations will come in handy. One tablespoon (T) is equal to 3 teaspoons (t) – hence, ⅓ T is equal to 1 t, and ½ T is equal to 1½ t. Roughly speaking, one imperial tablespoon is equal to 15 ml, and one teaspoon, 5 ml.

What's the best way to measure the ingredients?

For spices and small quantities of powder, measuring spoons are best. For almost all other ingredients, measuring by weight is easier and favours more consistent results.

Equivalent volume measures are also provided in a separate column on each recipe's facing page. Bear in mind, however, that if you use cups or spoons to measure ingredients in quantities greater than a few tablespoons, the amount so measured will not likely tally with the one given by weight.

Do the dry ingredients need to be sifted?

The use of a sifter to combine the flour with the baking powder, salt, and other dry ingredients as indicated insures that they will be evenly mixed together when added to the dough. For best results, pass the ingredients several times through the sifter. If you do not have a sifter, you can simply use a fine mesh strainer.

Any tips for rolling out the dough?

Dust the baking paper and dough with flour – or, for chocolate craquelins, a mixture of equal parts flour and cocoa powder. As you roll out the dough, continue dusting it with flour or the flour/cocoa mixture as needed, to keep it from sticking to the rolling pin and the paper. You can use the rolling pin as a support to gain easy access to the underside of the dough:

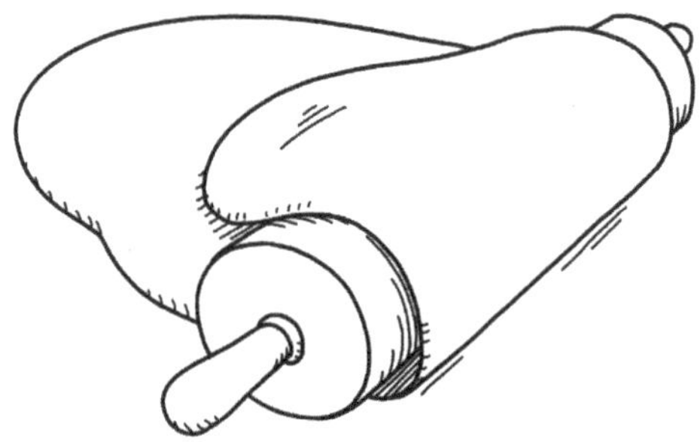

The recipes make enough dough, roughly speaking, to fill the usable area of a 40 x 32 cm (15¾" x 12½") baking sheet.

When do I add a topping or icing?

Prior to eventually cutting the dough, you can add a sprinkling of sea salt as desired to your savoury (or even sweet) craquelins; use the rolling pin to press the grains of salt into the dough and so fix them in place. The rolled-out dough can also be brushed with some water or vegan milk and sprinkled with an optional topping of your choice, such as seeds, rolled oats, bran...

Sugar-based icings are generally added prior to baking. In certain recipes, the instructions call for an icing to be added only after the dough has already been baked in the oven for 5 to 6 minutes.

To cut or not to cut?

As the Bard might say, *That is the question.* Presented as an enormously large and unbroken cracker or cookie, craquelins can make quite an impression. The question then becomes, *Who gets the fun of cracking and breaking them into pieces?* But craquelins are just as tasty when they've been cut into any number of shapes. All you need do is choose a motif…

Goban

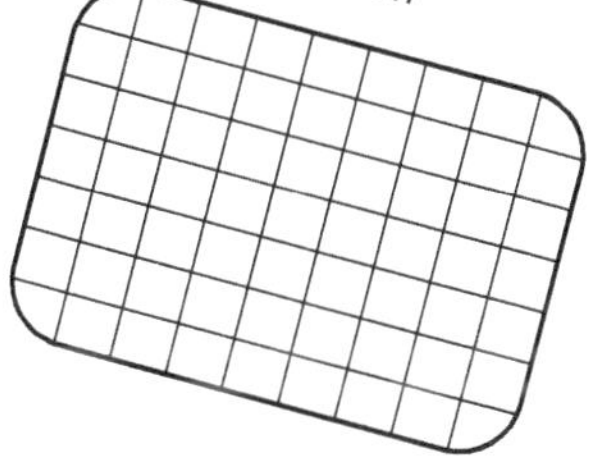

Manhattan

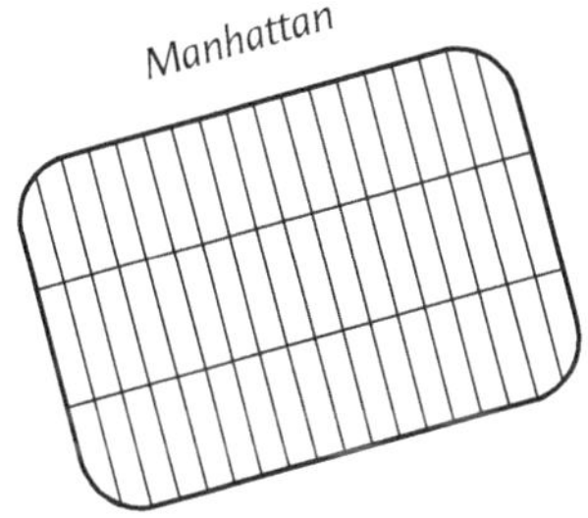

Bucky Fuller

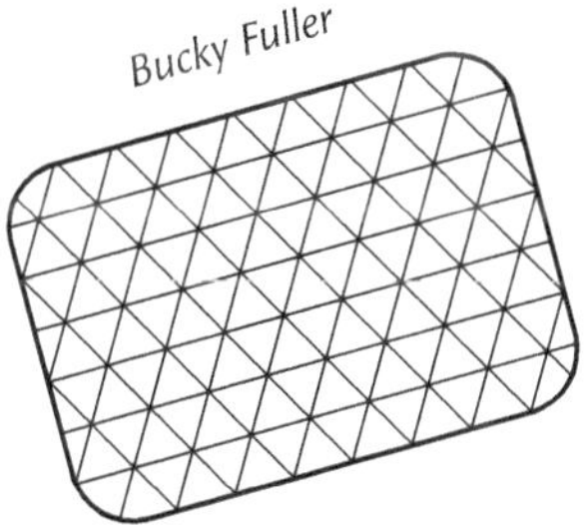

Harlequin

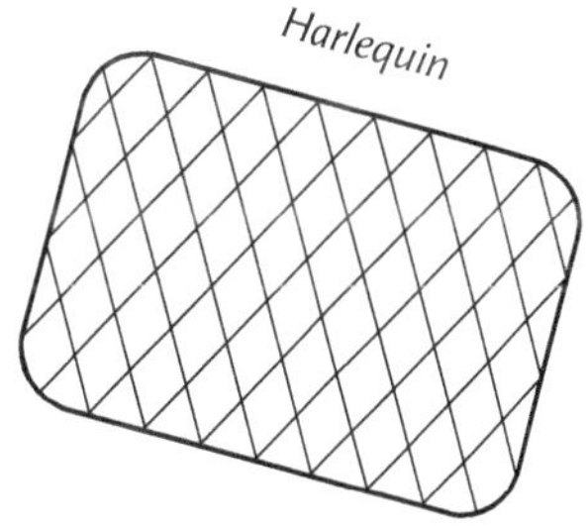

à la Valentina (IFR Enroute chart)

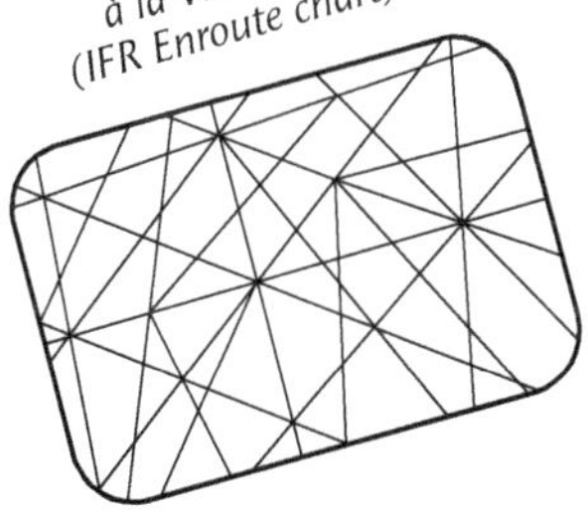

à la Hannah (bosons on the lam)

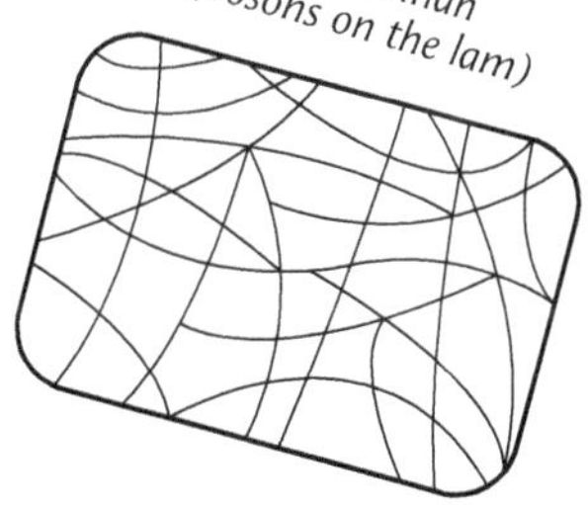

When is the best time to cut the dough?

For savoury craquelins, once you've rolled out the dough you can use a pizza cutter or a knife to cut the craquelin before baking, if you wish. Dipping the blade in some water first will help to keep it from sticking to the dough.

Sweet craquelins with no icing can also be cut beforehand, but it will be easier to cut them after 5 minutes of baking: the partially cooked dough, still easily cut, will better resist sticking to the blade. If an icing is added during baking, take the half-baked dough out of the oven and slide the baking paper off the baking sheet onto your work surface. Apply the icing; proceed with cutting if so desired – again, dipping the blade in some water to prevent sticking; then return the dough to the oven and continue baking as directed.

How long does it take to bake a craquelin?

The actual baking time is rather short: depending on the recipe, between 6 and 8 minutes at 180°C / 350°F / Gas mark 4, followed by a further 5 to 10 minutes with the thermostat set to 120°C / 250°F / Gas mark ½. It is useful to open the oven door briefly once or twice to allow steam to escape.

For the craquelin to then finish cooking and become dry and crunchy, it needs to cool completely. I obtain my best results by leaving the craquelin inside the oven on the baking sheet, with the door slightly ajar and the oven turned off.

Different ovens give different results, so these baking times are approximate. Try baking a few; you'll soon have a sense of how long it takes in your oven.

Although less precise for obtaining a perfectly crunchy outcome, there is another way to bake craquelins: turn the oven off after about 5 minutes and, keeping the oven door closed, leave the craquelin for several hours to finish cooking in the residual heat. It's a thrifty way to use your oven – especially if you've used it to bake some other dishes first.

How many servings can I count on, per recipe?

The nutritional tables at the end of the book are based on there being eight, ten, and sometimes twelve portions per recipe. Nevertheless, as my brother observes, *Your mileage may vary.* In short, it all depends.

What's the best way to store craquelins?

A metal biscuit or cookie tin is the best choice of container for keeping your leftover craquelins fresh and crunchy for several days at least.

Craquelins that become a bit soft and are no longer at their crunchy best can be rejuvenated by a short spell in the oven. Arrange them on a baking sheet and bake for ten minutes at 120°C / 250°F / Gas mark ½. Then, turn the oven off and leave them to cool completely with the oven door closed.

Can you use craquelin dough to make a quiche or pie crust?

Yes, and the results can be delicious. What's more, the possible combinations of doughs and fillings are almost endless...

Apart from certain exceptions, the recipes in this book make doughs that will be roughly 2 to 3 mm (≈ 1⁄16" to 1⁄8") thick, when rolled out to fill the usable area of a 40 x 32 cm (15¾" x 12½") baking sheet. As tart pans are generally smaller, a given recipe may provide a sufficient quantity of dough with which to line your pan. However, depending on how thick you want your crust to be, or to line a rather large tart pan, you may need to double the recipe in order to have enough dough for your needs.

Blind-bake the crust if your quiche or pie recipe calls for it.

Savoury

In France, the blends that are called *herbes de Provence* are made with several ingredients, the mainstay herbs being oregano, rosemary, thyme and savory. To these, most traditional recipes for the blend generally add at least one or more others: basil, chervil, tarragon, fennel seeds, hyssop, bay leaf, mint, parsley, sage...

In a culinary nod to Provence's reputation for being the lavender capital of the world, it has become fashionable of late – to the consternation of deep-dyed French purists – to add tiny purple lavender buds to the mix as well. As with everything, you'll have to decide: do you want to join the revolutionaries in their quest for change, or side with the reactionaries in defense of tradition?

or if you prefer...

2 T
3 T

1 T

1 T

14 T
½ t
¼ t

➛ For a topping, you can brush the rolled-out dough with a small amount of water and add a sprinkling of finely **diced onion**.

◇ HERBES DE PROVENCE ~ BLACK OLIVE

- Add **20 g** (2 T) pitted Greek-style **black olives**, finely chopped
- Reduce salt to ⅛ t

Herbes de Provence

20 g	**olive oil**	stir together in a bowl
45 g	**water**	
1 T	**herbes de Provence**	add and mix well
5 g	**malted yeast flakes**	add and mix well
100 g	**flour**	sift together, then add and mix well
½ t	**baking powder**	
¼ t	**salt**	

Preheat the oven with the baking sheet to 180°C / 350°F / Gas mark 4.

Roll out the dough, directly onto a sheet of baking paper.

Optional: you can sprinkle the dough with a few pinches of **sea salt**, fixing it in place with the rolling pin.

If desired, cut the dough before baking or after 5 minutes.

Bake for 7 minutes at 180°C, then reduce the thermostat to **120°C / 250°F / Gas mark ½** and continue baking with the oven door closed for 8 to 12 minutes. Then turn off the oven, open the door slightly and leave the craquelin inside, the time needed for it to become dry and crunchy as it cools completely.

or if you prefer...

With their mild yet distinctive wholegrain flavour, these craquelins go well with dips of all sorts.

2 T
3 T

2 T

➻ You can replace the wholewheat flour with one made from oats, spelt, barley, buckwheat, or some other grain, or use a mixture of different flours. Please note that craquelins made with flours that are gluten-free will be generally more compact.

14 T
½ t
¼ t

Wholewheat

20 g	**olive oil**	stir together in a bowl
45 g	**water**	
10 g	**malted yeast flakes**	add and mix well
100 g	**wholewheat flour**	sift together, then add and mix well
½ t	**baking powder**	
¼ t	**salt**	

Preheat the oven with the baking sheet to 180°C / 350°F / Gas mark 4.

Roll out the dough, directly onto a sheet of baking paper.

> Optional: you can sprinkle the dough with a few pinches of **sea salt**, fixing it in place with the rolling pin.
>
> If desired, cut the dough before baking or after 5 minutes.

Bake for 8 minutes at 180°C, then reduce the thermostat to **120°C / 250°F / Gas mark ½** and continue baking with the oven door closed for 8 to 12 minutes. Then turn off the oven, open the door slightly and leave the craquelin inside, the time needed for it to become dry and crunchy as it cools completely.

Pepperishly pleasant and with a bit of a bite, the flavour of these craquelins will vary according to the type of pepper you use – red, green, pink, black, or white.

There is a wild pepper from Madagascar that goes by the scientific name of *Piper borbonense* – and which is called *voatsiperifery* by the Malagasy – that is particularly tasty and worth trying.

◇ **CRACKED PEPPER ~ GARLIC**

- Using a mortar and pestle, crush **2 garlic cloves** (10 g) along with the salt from the recipe so as to obtain a viscous purée, then add this to the mixture of olive oil and water

◇ **CRACKED PEPPER ~ TURMERIC** or **CURRY**

- Add **1½ t** of powdered **turmeric** (curcuma) or **2 t** of **curry powder**

or if you prefer...

2 T
3 T
1 t
3 T
12½ T
½ t
¼ t

Cracked pepper

20 g	**olive oil**	stir together in a bowl
45 g	**water**	
1 t	**cracked pepper**	add and mix well
15 g	**malted yeast flakes**	add and mix well
90 g	**flour**	sift together, then add and mix well
½ t	**baking powder**	
¼ t	**salt**	

Preheat the oven with the baking sheet to 180°C / 350°F / Gas mark 4.

Roll out the dough, directly onto a sheet of baking paper.

Optional: you can sprinkle the dough with a few pinches of **sea salt**, fixing it in place with the rolling pin.

If desired, cut the dough before baking or after 5 minutes.

Bake for 7 minutes at 180°C, then reduce the thermostat to **120°C / 250°F / Gas mark ½** and continue baking with the oven door closed for 8 to 12 minutes. Then turn off the oven, open the door slightly and leave the craquelin inside, the time needed for it to become dry and crunchy as it cools completely.

or if you prefer...

→ For this recipe, you can make your own **thick tomato sauce**. Take a few 'Italian'-style tomatoes, either fresh or canned, and bring them to a low boil in a skillet or saucepan. Remove any skins, and continue cooking until enough water has evaporated to leave you with a thick, hearty sauce.

2 T
1⅓ T

2 T

1½ t
1 T

12½ T
½ t
¼ t
⅛ t

2⅓ T

Tomato ~ Black olive

20 g	**olive oil**	stir together in a bowl
20 g	**water**	
20 g	**Greek-style black olives**	remove stones, finely chop, and add
1½ t	**herbes de Provence**	add and mix well
5 g	**malted yeast flakes**	
90 g	**flour**	sift together, then add and mix well
½ t	**baking powder**	
¼ t	**sodium bicarbonate**	
⅛ t	**salt**	
35 g	**thick tomato sauce**	add the tomato sauce last and mix well

Preheat the oven with the baking sheet to 180°C / 350°F / Gas mark 4.

Roll out the dough, directly onto a sheet of baking paper.

Optional: you can sprinkle the dough with a few pinches of **sea salt**, fixing it in place with the rolling pin.

If desired, cut the dough before baking or after 5 minutes.

Bake for 7 minutes at 180°C, then reduce the thermostat to **120°C / 250°F / Gas mark ½** and continue baking with the oven door closed for 8 to 12 minutes. Then turn off the oven, open the door slightly and leave the craquelin inside, the time needed for it to become dry and crunchy as it cools completely.

or if you prefer...

Created in 1837 by two apothecaries, John Wheeley Lea and William Henry Perrins, the celebrated Worcestershire sauce is highly prized as a background flavour and a source of umami, one of the five fundamental flavours. For more about umami, see page 20.

➳ Anchovies feature in the original recipe for this archetypal English sauce, but vegan versions are readily available today. If you would like to make your own, you will find a vegan-friendly recipe on page 103.

2 T
1⅔ T

1 T
1 t

4 T

11 T
½ t
⅛ t
¼ t

Worcestershire

20 g	**olive oil**	stir together in a bowl
25 g	**water**	
15 g	**Worcestershire sauce**	add and mix well
5 g	**tamari** or soy sauce	
20 g	**malted yeast flakes**	add and mix well
80 g	**flour**	sift together, then add and mix well
½ t	**baking powder**	
⅛ t	**sodium bicarbonate**	
¼ t	**salt**	

Preheat the oven with the baking sheet to 180°C / 350°F / Gas mark 4.

Roll out the dough, directly onto a sheet of baking paper.

Optional: you can sprinkle the dough with a few pinches of **sea salt**, fixing it in place with the rolling pin.

If desired, cut the dough before baking or after 5 minutes.

Bake for 7 minutes at 180°C, then reduce the thermostat to **120°C / 250°F / Gas mark ½** and continue baking with the oven door closed for 8 to 12 minutes. Then turn off the oven, open the door slightly and leave the craquelin inside, the time needed for it to become dry and crunchy as it cools completely.

or if you prefer...

Malted yeast is both rich in certain B vitamins and a source of complete protein. What's more, it offers a deeply satisfying taste of umami, which is identified – along with sweet, salty, bitter, and sour – as being one of the five fundamental flavours (to which some add a sixth: spicy/pungent).

2 T
3 T

8 T

If vegans are inordinately fond of dried yeast flakes, it is because they satisfy the palate's craving for this unique umami flavour, which non-vegans so readily find in seafood, meat, and cheese.

8 T
½ t
¼ t

With a mild yet well-rounded flavour, these simple yeast craquelins go wonderfully well with dips of all sorts.

◇ MALTED YEAST ~ CHILI PEPPER

- Add 1 or 2 finely diced, **fresh chili peppers** – yellow, orange, red, or green

Leaving the flat bread
of what we know,
with the yeast of what we dream
may come to pass.

CLIVE BARKER

Malted yeast

20 g	**olive oil**	stir together in a bowl
45 g	**water**	
40 g	**malted yeast flakes**	add and mix well
60 g	**flour**	sift together, then add and mix well
½ t	**baking powder**	
¼ t	**salt**	

Preheat the oven with the baking sheet to 180°C / 350°F / Gas mark 4.

Roll out the dough, directly onto a sheet of baking paper.

Optional: you can sprinkle the dough with a few pinches of **sea salt**, fixing it in place with the rolling pin.

If desired, cut the dough before baking or after 5 minutes.

Bake for 7 minutes at 180°C, then reduce the thermostat to **120°C / 250°F / Gas mark ½** and continue baking with the oven door closed for 8 to 12 minutes. Then turn off the oven, open the door slightly and leave the craquelin inside, the time needed for it to become dry and crunchy as it cools completely.

or if you prefer...

This craquelin is inspired by French *sablés* and Scottish shortbreads, but it charts a different course by being savoury at heart. Intentionally thicker than most of the other craquelins featured in this book, it is both hearty and satisfying, making it a good choice for nibbles when supper on shore still seems a long ways off...

3 T
4⅔ T

3 T
8 T
4 T

1½ t

21 T
1 t
½ t

Savoury shortcrust

30 g	**olive oil**	}	stir together in a bowl
70 g	**water**		
15 g	**malted yeast flakes**	}	combine these ingredients and – with the aide of a mortar and pestle, a stick blender, or a food processor – grind them to a coarse meal and add to the above
60 g	**cashew nuts**		
30 g	**walnuts, almonds** and/or **hazelnuts**		
5 g	**sesame seeds** white, black, or both	}	lightly toast the sesame seeds in a dry skillet, then add and mix well
150 g	**flour**	}	sift together, then add and mix well
1 t	**baking powder**		
½ t	**salt**		

Preheat the oven with the baking sheet to 180 °C / 350 °F / Gas mark 4.

Roll out the dough, directly onto a sheet of baking paper. Note that the dough will be about twice as thick as most of the other craquelin doughs in this book.

Optional: you can sprinkle the dough with a few pinches of **sea salt**, fixing it in place with the rolling pin.

If desired, cut the dough before baking or after 5 minutes.

Bake for 8 minutes at 180 °C, then reduce the thermostat to **120 °C / 250 °F / Gas mark ½** and continue baking with the oven door closed for 8 to 12 minutes. Then turn off the oven, open the door slightly and leave the craquelin inside, the time needed for it to become dry and crunchy as it cools completely.

or if you prefer...

2 T

2⅔ T

2 T

1 T

11 T

½ t

¼ t

Lightly roasting or toasting the sesame seeds brings out their unique flavour. In a way, it's like whispering *'Open, sesame!'*

But a word to the wise: when heated, the little rascals tend to burst and jump out of the pan. The use of a lid will go a long ways to preventing unruly sesames from capering all over your kitchen...

➻ You can also use or mix in other seeds, such as cumin, hemp, flaxseed, poppy, sunflower, etc.

◇ SESAME ~ SMOKED PAPRIKA

- Start with **45 g** (3 T) of **water**
- Add and sift together with the flour and other dry ingredients **2 T** of **smoked paprika** – or, if you prefer, use a regular paprika, sweet, medium-hot, or hot, according to your taste

◇ POPPY SEED

- Omit the sesame seeds and add instead **20 g** (2 T) of **poppy seeds**

Sesame

20 g	**olive oil** or sesame seed oil		stir together in a bowl
40 g	**water**		
20 g	**sesame seeds** white, black, or both		lightly toast the sesame seeds in a dry skillet, then add and mix well
5 g	**malted yeast flakes**		add and mix well
80 g	**flour**		sift together, then add and mix well
½ t	**baking powder**		
¼ t	**salt**		

Preheat the oven with the baking sheet to 180°C / 350°F / Gas mark 4.

Roll out the dough, directly onto a sheet of baking paper.

Optional: you can sprinkle the dough with a few pinches of **sea salt**, fixing it in place with the rolling pin.

If desired, cut the dough before baking or after 5 minutes.

Bake for 7 minutes at 180°C, then reduce the thermostat to **120°C / 250°F / Gas mark ½** and continue baking with the oven door closed for 8 to 12 minutes. Then turn off the oven, open the door slightly and leave the craquelin inside, the time needed for it to become dry and crunchy as it cools completely.

or if you prefer...

Do five cloves of garlic seem like three or four too many? Well, have no fear: the antidote to vampires loses its bite when subjected to heat. In fact, spirited enthusiasts will likely slip in a few more, in honour of the proverb that says *As perfume is to the rose, so garlic is to health!*

Depending on your penchants and preferences, you can add to your dough 1 T fresh or 1 t dried herbs, such as chives, rosemary, or thyme.

2 T
2 T

≈ 5 cloves
¼ t

2 T

12½ T
½ t

Garlic ~ Sesame

20 g 30 g	**olive oil** **water**	stir together in a bowl
20 g ¼ t	**garlic** **salt**	using a mortar and pestle, crush the garlic with the salt to obtain a viscous mixture, then add and mix well
20 g	**sesame seeds** white, black, or both	lightly toast the sesame seeds in a dry skillet, then add and mix well
90 g ½ t	**flour** **baking powder**	sift together, then add and mix well

Preheat the oven with the baking sheet to 180°C / 350°F / Gas mark 4.

Roll out the dough, directly onto a sheet of baking paper.

Optional: you can sprinkle the dough with a few pinches of **sea salt**, fixing it in place with the rolling pin.

If desired, cut the dough before baking or after 5 minutes.

Bake for 7 minutes at 180°C, then reduce the thermostat to **120°C / 250°F / Gas mark ½** and continue baking with the oven door closed for 8 to 12 minutes. Then turn off the oven, open the door slightly and leave the craquelin inside, the time needed for it to become dry and crunchy as it cools completely.

or if you prefer...

With their mild yet distinctive flavour, these craquelins go well with dips of all sorts.

Please note that since chickpea flour does not contain gluten, these craquelins are a bit more compact than those that are made with only wheat flour.

2 T
2⅔ T

9½ T
4 T
½ t
¼ t

◇ **CHICKPEA ~ CHIA** or **POPPY SEED**

- Add **10 g** (1 T) of **chia seeds** or **poppy seeds**

◇ **CHICKPEA ~ MALTED YEAST**

- Start with **40 g** (2⅔ T) of **water**
- Reduce by 10 g the quantity of each flour, and in their place add **20 g** (4 T) of **malted yeast flakes**

◇ **CHICKPEA ~ GARLIC**

- Add **1 t** of **granulated garlic** or **½** to **¾ t** of **garlic powder** to the flour mixture

◇ **CHICKPEA ~ SESAME**

- Add **20 g** (2 T) of either white or black **sesame seeds**, or a mix of both, lightly toasted in a dry skillet beforehand

Chickpea

20 g	**olive oil**	stir together in a bowl
40 g	**water**	
70 g	**chickpea flour**	sift together, then add and mix well
30 g	**wheat flour**	
½ t	**baking powder**	
¼ t	**salt**	

Preheat the oven with the baking sheet to 180°C / 350°F / Gas mark 4.

Roll out the dough, directly onto a sheet of baking paper.

Optional: you can sprinkle the dough with a few pinches of **sea salt**, fixing it in place with the rolling pin.

If desired, cut the dough before baking or after 5 minutes.

Bake for 7 minutes at 180°C, then reduce the thermostat to **120°C / 250°F / Gas mark ½** and continue baking with the oven door closed for 10 to 15 minutes. Then turn off the oven, open the door slightly and leave the craquelin inside, the time needed for it to become dry and crunchy as it cools completely.

or if you prefer...

2 T
2⅓ T
1 T
1½ t
11 T
2 t
½ t
¼ t

What we call chili powder is usually a mix of several herbs and spices. In addition to chili peppers – of which several varieties are sometimes used, including peppers that are hot and spicy – chili powders generally contain one or more of the following: paprika, garlic, onion, cumin, oregano, cloves...

➳ You can create a wholly different craquelin by replacing the chili powder with a different **spice blend**, of which there are many from around the world from which to choose, their names alone an invitation to explore new horizons: *Cajun... ras el-hanout... hawaij... berbéré... za'atar... colombo... tandoori masala... shichimi tōgarashi...*

Tes citrons viennent du Maroc
Tes litchis de Madagascar
Tes piments du Sénégal
Tes mangues viennent du Bangui
Tes noix d'coco d'Côte d'Ivoire
Tes ananas d'Californie

Et tu reproches à ton voisin d'être un étranger

Julos Beaucarne

Chili

20 g	**olive oil**	stir together in a bowl
35 g	**water**	
5 g	**malted yeast flakes**	add and mix well
5 g	**rapadura sugar**	
80 g	**flour**	sift together, then add and mix well
2 t	**chili powder**	
½ t	**baking powder**	
¼ t	**salt**	

Preheat the oven with the baking sheet to 180°C / 350°F / Gas mark 4.

Roll out the dough, directly onto a sheet of baking paper.

Optional: you can sprinkle the dough with a few pinches of **sea salt**, fixing it in place with the rolling pin.

For a savoury-sweet result, you can also brush the dough with a bit of water and then add a light sprinkling of **blond cane sugar**.

If desired, cut the dough before baking or after 5 minutes.

Bake for 7 minutes at 180°C, then reduce the thermostat to **120°C / 250°F / Gas mark ½** and continue baking with the oven door closed for 8 to 12 minutes. Then turn off the oven, open the door slightly and leave the craquelin inside, the time needed for it to become dry and crunchy as it cools completely.

or if you prefer...

2 T
2⅔ T
1 T
1 T
11 T
2 to 3 t
½ t
¼ t

Like chili powder, curry powder is a mixture of several ingredients, with different curry powders each having their own particular flavour.

Among the herbs and spices generally used in its preparation, one finds coriander, cumin, mustard, turmeric, chili, pepper, fenugreek, cardamom, cloves, ginger, fennel, garlic, onion...

➳ According to your tastes, you can enhance the flavour of a curry powder by adding a few pinches of freshly ground cardamom, cinnamon, clove...

Curry ~ Sesame

20 g	**olive oil**	}	stir together in a bowl
40 g	**water**		
10 g	**sesame seeds** white, black, or both	}	lightly toast the sesame seeds in a dry skillet, then add and mix well
5 g	**malted yeast flakes**	}	add and mix well
80 g	**flour**	}	sift together, then add and mix well
2 to 3 t	**curry powder**		
½ t	**baking powder**		
¼ t	**salt**		

Preheat the oven with the baking sheet to 180°C / 350°F / Gas mark 4.

Roll out the dough, directly onto a sheet of baking paper.

Optional: you can sprinkle the dough with a few pinches of **sea salt**, fixing it in place with the rolling pin.

If desired, cut the dough before baking or after 5 minutes.

Bake for 7 minutes at 180°C, then reduce the thermostat to **120°C / 250°F / Gas mark ½** and continue baking with the oven door closed for 8 to 12 minutes. Then turn off the oven, open the door slightly and leave the craquelin inside, the time needed for it to become dry and crunchy as it cools completely.

or if you prefer...

Omnipresent in the Land of the Rising Sun, gomashio is often used as a condiment to be served with rice.

½ t
5 T

➳ Please note that most gomashios have a ratio of salt to sesame that is much higher than the ratio given in this recipe, where the proportion of salt is considerably reduced.

Note too that compared to the other craquelins in this book, these tend to be somewhat crumbly, due to the dough having proportionally less flour.

2 T
2⅔ T

8 T
½ t

◆ **GOMASHIO ~ SEAWEED**

- Soak **5 g** (3 T) of **dried seaweed** for 10 minutes in **45 g** (3 T) of **water**, and use this in place of the recipe's 40 g of water

Les algues entr'ouvraient leurs âpres cassolettes
D'où montait une odeur de phosphore et de sel,
Et, jetant leurs reflets empourprés vers le ciel,
Semblaient, au fond des eaux, des lits de violettes.

Renée Vivien

Gomashio

To begin with, prepare the **gomashio** with sesame seeds and sea salt

½ t	**sea salt**	heat the salt in a dry skillet, then add and toast the seeds; transfer the mixture while still very hot to a mortar and finely grind the seeds
50 g	**sesame seeds** white, black, or a mixture	

Following this, prepare the dough

20 g	**olive oil**	stir the oil and water together in a bowl, then add the **gomashio** and mix well
40 g	**water**	
60 g	**flour**	sift together, then add and mix well
½ t	**baking powder**	

Preheat the oven with the baking sheet to 180°C / 350°F / Gas mark 4.

Roll out the dough, directly onto a sheet of baking paper.

Optional: you can sprinkle the dough with a few pinches of **sea salt**, fixing it in place with the rolling pin.

If desired, cut the dough before baking or after 5 minutes.

Bake for 7 minutes at 180°C, then reduce the thermostat to **120°C / 250°F / Gas mark ½** and continue baking with the oven door closed for 8 to 12 minutes. Then turn off the oven, open the door slightly and leave the craquelin inside, the time needed for it to become dry and crunchy as it cools completely.

or if you prefer...

Sambar powder, or *sambar masala,* is traditionally used to prepare a dish that is native to southern India and Sri Lanka, and which is made with either lentils or pigeon peas.

Although sambar powder resembles curry powder and is used in much the same way, it nevertheless confers a very different flavour. There is no set recipe for *sambar masala,* but it generally contains a number of these ingredients: chickpeas, split peas, lentils, asa foetida, cinnamon, coconut, coriander, cumin, turmeric, curry leaves, fenugreek, black mustard, black pepper, hot chili peppers...

2 T
3 T

2½ T*
1 T

1 T

11 T
1 T
½ t
¼ t

* *packed*

Sambar

20 g	**olive oil**	stir together in a bowl
45 g	**water**	
20 g	**ground almonds**	add and mix well
10 g	**blond and brown flaxseeds** (also called linseeds)	
10 g	**sesame seeds** white, black, or both	lightly toast the sesame seeds in a dry skillet, then add and mix well
80 g	**flour**	sift together, then add and mix well
1 T	**sambar powder**	
½ t	**baking powder**	
¼ t	**salt**	

Preheat the oven with the baking sheet to 180°C / 350°F / Gas mark 4.

Roll out the dough, directly onto a sheet of baking paper.

Optional: you can sprinkle the dough with a few pinches of **sea salt**, fixing it in place with the rolling pin.

If desired, cut the dough before baking or after 5 minutes.

Bake for 7 minutes at 180°C, then reduce the thermostat to **120°C / 250°F / Gas mark ½** and continue baking with the oven door closed for 8 to 12 minutes. Then turn off the oven, open the door slightly and leave the craquelin inside, the time needed for it to become dry and crunchy as it cools completely.

or if you prefer...

These maritime-flavoured craquelins appeal to just about everyone. Even my youngest daughter, who is reluctant to try anything that is green and possibly good for her health, tells me they are one of her favourites...

3 T

3 T

2 T

➳ You can use **a blend of seaweeds**, or opt for a single seaweed of your choice (dulse, nori, sea lettuce, wakame...)

2 T

◇ **SEAWEED WITH WASABI ICING**

11 T
½ t
⅛ t

- After baking for 4 to 5 minutes, remove the dough from the oven and brush with a mixture of

10 g (1½ t) of **wasabi paste**
15 g (1 T) of **vegan milk**
15 g (1¼ T, packed) of **icing sugar**

Proceed with cutting the dough at this point if desired, then return the dough to the oven and continue baking as directed.

Call us not weeds – we are flowers of the Sea
For lovely and bright and gay tinted are we
And quite independent of sunshine or showers
Oh call us not weeds – we are ocean's gay flowers

AUTHOR UNKNOWN

Seaweed

5 g	**dried seaweed**	finely chop the seaweed
45 g	**water**	put the water in a bowl, add the seaweed and let soak 10 minutes
20 g	**olive oil**	add and stir well
20 g	**sesame seeds** white, black, or both	lightly toast the sesame seeds in a dry skillet, then add and mix well
80 g ½ t ⅛ t	**flour** **baking powder** **salt**	sift together, then add and mix well

Preheat the oven with the baking sheet to 180°C / 350°F / Gas mark 4.

Roll out the dough, directly onto a sheet of baking paper.

Optional: you can sprinkle the dough with a few pinches of **sea salt**, fixing it in place with the rolling pin.

If desired, cut the dough before baking or after 5 minutes.

Bake for 7 minutes at 180°C, then reduce the thermostat to **120°C / 250°F / Gas mark ½** and continue baking with the oven door closed for 8 to 12 minutes. Then turn off the oven, open the door slightly and leave the craquelin inside, the time needed for it to become dry and crunchy as it cools completely.

or if you prefer...

Like the wish-fulfilling *Kalpavriksha* or 'world tree' of the Vedic scriptures, the coconut palm deserves humankind's gratitude for all that it bestows. It is a source of food; of drinkable water and cooking oil; of firewood and charcoal, thatch and timber; of strong coir fibre; of leaves that we weave into baskets; of shells that serve to make bowls and utensils, buttons and jewellery. For its usefulness and beauty, there are few plants on Earth that can rival this ubiquitous emblem of the tropics.

1½ T
4 T

3½ T

1 T

11 T
2 to 3 t
½ t
¼ t

Coconut ~ Curry

15 g	**olive oil**	stir together in a bowl
60 g	**coconut milk**	
25 g	**shredded coconut,** unsweetened	add and mix well
5 g	**malted yeast flakes**	add and mix well
80 g	**flour**	sift together, then add and mix well
2 to 3 t	**curry powder**	
½ t	**baking powder**	
¼ t	**salt**	

Preheat the oven with the baking sheet to 180°C / 350°F / Gas mark 4.

Roll out the dough, directly onto a sheet of baking paper.

Optional: you can sprinkle the dough with a few pinches of **sea salt**, fixing it in place with the rolling pin.

If desired, cut the dough before baking or after 5 minutes.

Bake for 7 minutes at 180°C, then reduce the thermostat to **120°C / 250°F / Gas mark ½** and continue baking with the oven door closed for 8 to 12 minutes. Then turn off the oven, open the door slightly and leave the craquelin inside, the time needed for it to become dry and crunchy as it cools completely.

Sweet

For these craquelins, you can use hazelnuts that have already been finely ground, or grind whole hazelnuts to a fine meal yourself using a mortar and pestle, a stick blender, or a food processor. You can also lightly roast the hazelnuts beforehand, to enhance their flavour.

◇ WALNUT

- Replace the hazelnuts with **walnuts**
- Use **40 g** (3 T) of **blond cane sugar** and omit the rapadura sugar

◇ PECAN

- Replace the hazelnuts with **pecans**

◇ PINE NUT

- Replace the hazelnuts with **pine nuts**
- Use **40 g** (3 T) of **blond cane sugar** and omit the rapadura sugar

or if you prefer...

1 T

2⅓ T

5 T*

1¾ T
1⅓ T*
½ t

8 T
½ t
⅛ t

** packed*

Hazelnut

20 g	**almond butter** or hazelnut butter	stir together in a bowl
35 g	**vegan milk**	
40 g	**ground hazelnuts**	add and mix well
25 g	**blond cane sugar**	add and mix well
15 g	**rapadura sugar**	
½ t	**vanilla sugar** or extract	
60 g	**flour**	sift together, then add and mix well
½ t	**baking powder**	
⅛ t	**salt**	

Preheat the oven with the baking sheet to 180°C / 350°F / Gas mark 4.

Roll out the dough, directly onto a sheet of baking paper.

Optional: you can brush the dough with a bit of **vegan milk** or water and then add a light sprinkling of **blond cane sugar** and/or chopped **hazelnuts** that have been lightly toasted in a dry skillet, using the rolling pin to lightly press them into the dough.

If desired, cut the dough after 5 minutes of baking.

Bake for 6 minutes at 180°C, then reduce the thermostat to **120°C / 250°F / Gas mark ½** and continue baking with the oven door closed for 5 to 10 minutes. Then turn off the oven, open the door slightly and leave the craquelin inside, the time needed for it to become dry and crunchy as it cools completely.

or if you prefer...

Coffee icing

For a touch of added sweetness, you can brush the dough prior to baking with some leftover **coffee-flavoured vegan milk** and then add if desired a sprinkling of **blond cane sugar**, **cocoa**, and/or **cinnamon.**

1 to 3 T
6 T

Alternatively, for a completely different result, you can brush the dough with a mixture of **coffee-flavoured vegan milk** and **icing sugar**.

1 T
2 T

3 T

◇ CAFÉ AU CHOCOLAT

½ t

- After 5 minutes of baking, add a **drizzled dark chocolate icing** per the instructions given on page 60

11 T
½ t
⅛ t

Coffee

→ To begin with, prepare the **coffee-flavoured vegan milk**

5 to 15 g	**ground coffee**	heat the vegan milk in a small saucepan; add the ground coffee, and let the mixture brew for 5 minutes; strain and use in next step
90 g	**oat milk** – *or other vegan milk that does not curdle when heated*	
20 g	**almond butter**	stir together in a bowl
30 g	**coffee-flavoured vegan milk**	
40 g	**blond cane sugar**	add and mix well
½ t	**vanilla sugar** or extract	
80 g	**flour**	sift together, then add and mix well
½ t	**baking powder**	
⅛ t	**salt**	

Preheat the oven with the baking sheet to 180°C / 350°F / Gas mark 4.

Roll out the dough, directly onto a sheet of baking paper.

Optional: you can brush the dough quite simply with some leftover **coffee-flavoured vegan milk**.

Or, you can add a **coffee icing** (page opposite), and if desired, cut the dough after 5 minutes of baking.

Bake for 6 minutes at 180°C, then reduce the thermostat to **120°C / 250°F / Gas mark ½** and continue baking with the oven door closed for 5 to 10 minutes. Then turn off the oven, open the door slightly and leave the craquelin inside, the time needed for it to become dry and crunchy as it cools completely.

or if you prefer...

1½ T
3⅓ T
1¾ T
2 T*
½ t
8 T
3 T
2 T
2 T
14 T
½ t
⅛ t
⅛ t

** packed*

These rolled-oat craquelins are thicker than most of the other craquelins featured in this book. They also have a softer centre. If you prefer them dry and crisp, add 2 to 3 minutes more to their baking time at 180°C, before reducing the thermostat to 120°C.

➛ Many other **seeds and dried fruits** can be added, or used in place of those mentioned in the recipe...

- almonds
- chia seeds
- flaxseeds (linseeds)
- hazelnuts
- pecans
- quinoa
- sesame seeds
- walnuts

- apricots
- cranberries
- dates
- figs
- mango
- pineapple
- prunes
- raspberries

Jeg er Havren. Jeg har Bjælder paa;
mer end tyve, tror jeg, paa hvert Straa.
Bonden kalder dem for mine Fold.
Gud velsigne ham, den Bondeknold!

JEPPE AAKJÆR

Rolled oats

30 g	**almond butter**	stir together in a bowl
50 g	**vegan milk**	
25 g	**blond cane sugar**	add and mix well
25 g	**rapadura sugar**	
½ t	**vanilla sugar** or extract	
50 g	**rolled oats**	first cut the raisins or sultanas into smaller pieces, then add these ingredients and mix well
30 g	**raisins** or sultanas	
20 g	**sunflower seeds**	
20 g	**pumpkin seeds**	
100 g	**flour**	sift together, then add and mix well
½ t	**baking powder**	
⅛ t	**sodium bicarbonate**	
⅛ t	**salt**	

Preheat the oven with the baking sheet to 180 °C / 350 °F / Gas mark 4.

Roll out the dough, directly onto a sheet of baking paper. Note that the dough will be about twice as thick as most of the other craquelin doughs in this book.

Optional: you can brush the dough with a bit of **vegan milk** or water and then add a light sprinkling of **blond cane sugar**.

If desired, cut the dough after 5 minutes of baking.

Bake for 6 minutes at 180 °C, then reduce the thermostat to **120 °C / 250 °F / Gas mark ½** and continue baking with the oven door closed for 5 to 10 minutes. Then turn off the oven, open the door slightly and leave the craquelin inside, the time needed for it to become dry and crunchy as it cools completely.

or if you prefer...

My ancestors by the name of GILLIES hailed from Scotland, which is likely why I tried my hand at playing bagpipes in my youth. To be honest, my grace notes were all fingers and thumbs. But if the day ever comes that I find myself trekking 'cross the Highlands, dressed in a kilt and bagpipes a-blowing, I reckon a stash of shortbread-inspired craquelins will be a welcome treat to find tucked away in my sporran...

1½ T
4⅔ T

8 T
4 T

1½ t

5¾ T
1 t

21 T
1 t
¼ t

Shortbread

30 g	**almond butter**	stir together in a bowl
70 g	**vegan milk**	
60 g	**cashew nuts**	combine these ingredients and – with the aide of a mortar and pestle, a stick blender, or a food processor – grind them to a coarse meal and add to the above
30 g	**walnuts, almonds** and/or **hazelnuts**	
5 g	**sesame seeds** white, black, or both	lightly toast the sesame seeds in a dry skillet, then add and mix well
80 g	**blond cane sugar**	add and mix well
1 t	**vanilla sugar** or extract	
150 g	**flour**	sift together, then add and mix well
1 t	**baking powder**	
¼ t	**salt**	

Preheat the oven with the baking sheet to 180°C / 350°F / Gas mark 4.

Roll out the dough, directly onto a sheet of baking paper. Note that the dough will be about twice as thick as most of the other craquelin doughs in this book.

If desired, cut the dough after 5 minutes of baking.

Bake for 6 minutes at 180°C, or for 8 to 9 minutes if you wish them to be baked all the way through; then reduce the thermostat to **120°C / 250°F / Gas mark ½** and continue baking with the oven door closed for 5 to 10 minutes. Turn off the oven, open the door slightly and leave the craquelin inside, the time needed for it to become softly crunchy as it cools completely.

or if you prefer...

◆ **COCONUT ~ DRIZZLED DARK CHOCOLATE ICING**

1 T
2⅔ T

- After 5 minutes of baking, add a **drizzled dark chocolate icing** per the instructions given on page 60

4 T*

Optional: sprinkle the top with **shredded coconut**.

◆ **COCONUT ~ ORANGE**

3 T
½ t

- Reduce the coconut milk by 15 g (1 T)
- Add **5 to 10 g** (1 to 2 T) of **orange zest** (≈ ½ to 1 orange)
- After mixing in the flour, add **15 g** (1 T) of **concentrated orange juice** (see p. 58)

8 T
½ t
⅛ t

Optional: just prior to reducing the thermostat, sprinkle the half-baked dough with **20 g** (¾ oz or 2 T) of **chocolate chips**, or squares of dark chocolate that have been chopped into small pieces.

** packed*

◆ **CHOCOLATE ~ COCONUT**

- Start with **45 g** (3 T) of **coconut milk**
- Add **15 g** (½ oz) of **dark chocolate**, finely grated
- Reduce the flour by 10 g (1½ T) and replace it with **10 g** (1½ T) of **cocoa powder**

Optional: after 5 minutes of baking, add a **drizzled dark chocolate icing** per the instructions given on page 60 and, if desired, sprinkle the top with **shredded coconut**.

Coconut

20 g	**almond butter**	stir together in a bowl
40 g	**coconut milk**	
25 g	**shredded coconut**, unsweetened	add and mix well
40 g	**blond cane sugar**	add and mix well
½ t	**vanilla sugar** or extract	
60 g	**flour**	sift together, then add and mix well
½ t	**baking powder**	
⅛ t	**salt**	

Preheat the oven with the baking sheet to 180°C / 350°F / Gas mark 4.

Roll out the dough, directly onto a sheet of baking paper.

Optional: you can brush the dough with a bit of **vegan milk** or **coconut milk** or water and then add a light sprinkling of **blond cane sugar.**

If desired, cut the dough after 5 minutes of baking.

Bake for 6 minutes at 180°C, then reduce the thermostat to **120°C / 250°F / Gas mark ½** and continue baking with the oven door closed for 5 to 10 minutes. Then turn off the oven, open the door slightly and leave the craquelin inside, the time needed for it to become dry and crunchy as it cools completely.

or if you prefer...

1 T
2⅓ T

2 T*
½ oz

3 T
½ t

7¼ T
2 T
½ t
⅛ t

** packed*

➻ Delicious as is, this craquelin also lends itself to many **variations**...

The faint note of almond can be made stronger by adding ¼ to ½ t of **bitter almond essence**.

You can sprinkle the top with **chocolate chips** just prior to reducing the thermostat, or add a **drizzled dark chocolate icing** (see p. 60).

For a mocha version, use **coffee-flavoured vegan milk** (see p. 47).

A green tea version can be made by adding 2 to 3 t of **matcha tea** to the flour mixture, and if desired either a matcha tea icing (see p. 90) or a dark chocolate icing (see p. 60) to which may be added 1 to 2 t of matcha tea.

Another variation that can be surprising but has its devotees is made by adding an icing made with **wasabi** (see p. 84).

◇ CHOCOLATE ~ QUINOA

- Add **10 g** (1 T) of coarsely ground **quinoa seeds**
- Opt for a mixture of **25 g** (1¾ T) of **blond cane sugar** and **15 g** (1⅓ T, packed) of **rapadura sugar**

◇ CHOCOLATE ~ ESPELETTE PEPPER

- Add **⅛** to **½ t** of ground **Espelette pepper** to the flour, depending on how spicy you want your craquelin to be

  Optional: after rolling out the dough, first brush it with **vegan milk** or water, then sprinkle with ground **Espelette pepper** – and, if desired, **blond cane sugar**.

Chocolate

20 g	**almond butter**	stir together in a bowl
35 g	**vegan milk**	
15 g	**ground almonds**	add and mix well
15 g	**dark chocolate**, finely grated	
40 g	**blond cane sugar**	add and mix well
½ t	**vanilla sugar** or extract	
50 g	**flour**	sift together, then add and mix well
15 g	**cocoa powder**	
½ t	**baking powder**	
⅛ t	**salt**	

Preheat the oven with the baking sheet to 180°C / 350°F / Gas mark 4.

Using a mixture of **flour** and **cocoa powder** to prevent sticking (see p. 4), roll out the dough, directly onto a sheet of baking paper.

Optional: you can sprinkle the dough with a few pinches of **sea salt**, fixing it in place with the rolling pin, or you can brush the dough with a bit of **vegan milk** or water and then add a light sprinkling of **blond cane sugar**, **cinnamon**, and/or **cocoa**.

If desired, cut the dough after 5 minutes of baking.

Bake for 6 minutes at 180°C, then reduce the thermostat to **120°C / 250°F / Gas mark ½** and continue baking with the oven door closed for 5 to 10 minutes. Then turn off the oven, open the door slightly and leave the craquelin inside, the time needed for it to become dry and crunchy as it cools completely.

◇ CHOCOLATE ~ MINT ~ DRIZZLED MINT CHOCOLATE ICING

In a small saucepan over very low heat, or in a double boiler, melt **40 g** (1½ oz) of **dark chocolate**. To this, add **5 to 10 drops** (⅛ to ¼ t) of **peppermint oil**.

After 5 minutes of baking, remove the dough from the oven and slide the baking paper off the baking sheet onto your work surface. Using a spoon or spatula – and with a nod to the artist Jackson Pollock – drip or drizzle the melted mint chocolate onto the half-baked dough. If so desired, proceed with cutting the dough with a pizza cutter or knife dipped in water, then return the half-baked dough to the oven and continue baking as directed.

Alternatively, you can **double** the amount of mint chocolate and, with the aide of the flat side of a bowl scraper, a spatula or a pastry brush, spread the melted chocolate evenly over the entire top surface.

➛ Please note that peppermint oil, like all essential oils, is volatile, and should be handled with caution –

- To protect your eyes and lungs from the vapours it gives off when heated, avoid having your face too close to the oven door when you open it
- To insure the peppermint flavour is not transferred to other craquelins, it is best to bake and store your mint chocolate craquelins separately

or if you prefer...

1 T
2⅓ T

1⁄16 t

2 T*
½ oz

3 T
½ t

7¼ T
2 T
½ t
⅛ t

** packed*

Chocolate ~ Mint

20 g	**almond butter**	stir together in a bowl
35 g	**vegan milk**	
5 drops *or more, as desired*	**peppermint oil**	add and mix well
15 g	**ground almonds**	add and mix well
15 g	**dark chocolate**, finely grated	
40 g	**blond cane sugar**	add and mix well
½ t	**vanilla sugar** or extract	
50 g	**flour**	sift together, then add and mix well
15 g	**cocoa powder**	
½ t	**baking powder**	
⅛ t	**salt**	

Preheat the oven with the baking sheet to 180 °C / 350 °F / Gas mark 4.

Using a mixture of **flour** and **cocoa powder** to prevent sticking (see p. 4), roll out the dough, directly onto a sheet of baking paper.

If desired, cut the dough after 5 minutes of baking.

Bake for 6 minutes at 180 °C, then reduce the thermostat to **120 °C / 250 °F / Gas mark ½** and continue baking with the oven door closed for 5 to 10 minutes. Then turn off the oven, open the door slightly and leave the craquelin inside, the time needed for it to become dry and crunchy as it cools completely.

➸ You can make your own **concentrated orange juice**. Once you have grated the orange peel to obtain the zest, halve and squeeze the orange to obtain the juice – if you plan to add the icing, start with the juice of 2 oranges. Bring the juice to a boil in a small saucepan, then lower the heat and reduce the liquid by three-quarters.

For a slightly stronger orange flavour, you can replace the vegan milk with additional concentrated orange juice, or add 1 t **orange blossom water**.

Orange icing

For a touch of added sweetness, brush the dough prior to baking with 1 T or more of **concentrated orange juice** and then add a light sprinkling of **blond cane sugar**.

◇ CHOCOLATE ~ ORANGE ~ DRIZZLED DARK CHOCOLATE ICING

- After 5 minutes of baking, add a **drizzled dark chocolate icing** per the instructions given on page 60

◇ CHOCOLATE ~ LEMON

- Replace the orange zest with **lemon zest** (≈ ½ to 1 lemon)
- Replace the concentrated orange juice with **concentrated lemon juice** (see p. 72)

  If you opt to add an icing, brush the rolled-out dough with **freshly squeezed lemon juice**, then sprinkle with **blond cane sugar**.

or if you prefer...

1 T
1⅓ T

2 T*
½ oz
1 to 2 T

3 T
½ t

8 T
2 T
½ t
⅛ t
⅛ t

1 T

** packed*

Chocolate ~ Orange

20 g	**almond butter**	stir together in a bowl
20 g	**vegan milk**	
15 g	**ground almonds**	add and mix well
15 g	**dark chocolate**, finely grated	
5 to 10 g	**orange zest** (≈ ½ to 1 orange)	
40 g	**blond cane sugar**	add and mix well
½ t	**vanilla sugar** or extract	
60 g	**flour**	sift together, then add and mix well
15 g	**cocoa powder**	
½ t	**baking powder**	
⅛ t	**sodium bicarbonate**	
⅛ t	**salt**	
15 g	**concentrated orange juice**	add the juice last and mix well

Preheat the oven with the baking sheet to 180 °C / 350 °F / Gas mark 4.

Using a mixture of **flour** and **cocoa powder** to prevent sticking (see p. 4), roll out the dough, directly onto a sheet of baking paper.

> Optional: add an **orange icing** (page opposite). If desired, cut the dough after 5 minutes of baking.

Bake for 6 minutes at 180 °C, then reduce the thermostat to **120 °C / 250 °F / Gas mark ½** and continue baking with the oven door closed for 5 to 10 minutes. Then turn off the oven, open the door slightly and leave the craquelin inside, the time needed for it to become dry and crunchy as it cools completely.

◆ CHOCOLATE ~ INTENSELY SO ~ DRIZZLED DARK CHOCOLATE ICING

In a small saucepan over very low heat, or in a double boiler, melt **40 g** (1½ oz) of **dark chocolate**.

After 5 minutes of baking, remove the dough from the oven and slide the baking paper off the baking sheet onto your work surface. Using a spoon or spatula – and with a nod to the artist Jackson Pollock – drip or drizzle the melted chocolate onto the half-baked dough. If so desired, proceed with cutting the dough with a pizza cutter or knife dipped in water, then return the half-baked dough to the oven and continue baking as directed.

Alternatively, for a uniform **dark chocolate icing**, you can **double** the amount of chocolate and, with the aide of the flat side of a bowl scraper, a spatula or a pastry brush, spread the melted chocolate evenly over the entire top surface.

or if you prefer...

1 T
2⅔ T

2 T*
½ oz

3 T
½ t

7¼ T
3 T
½ t
⅛ t

** packed*

Chocolate ~ Intensely so

20 g	**almond butter**	stir together in a bowl
40 g	**vegan milk**	
15 g	**ground almonds**	add and mix well
15 g	**dark chocolate**, at least **70%** **cacao**, finely grated	
40 g	**blond cane sugar**	add and mix well
½ t	**vanilla sugar** or extract	
50 g	**flour**	sift together, then add and mix well
20 g	**cocoa powder**	
½ t	**baking powder**	
⅛ t	**salt**	

Preheat the oven with the baking sheet to 180°C / 350°F / Gas mark 4.

Using a mixture of **flour** and **cocoa powder** to prevent sticking (see p. 4), roll out the dough, directly onto a sheet of baking paper.

Optional: you can sprinkle the dough with a few pinches of **sea salt**, fixing it in place with the rolling pin, or you can brush the dough with a bit of **vegan milk** or water and then add a light sprinkling of **blond cane sugar**, **cinnamon**, and/or **cocoa**.

If desired, cut the dough after 5 minutes of baking.

Bake for 6 minutes at 180°C, then reduce the thermostat to **120°C / 250°F / Gas mark ½** and continue baking with the oven door closed for 5 to 10 minutes. Then turn off the oven, open the door slightly and leave the craquelin inside, the time needed for it to become dry and crunchy as it cools completely.

Popular throughout the Commonwealth, the ginger nut biscuit owes its nominal modifier to the fact that it's as 'hard as a nut' – and a good thing, too: it's what keeps it from falling apart when dipped into tea!

Being a good deal thinner, this craquelin version might not be as hardy as your average ginger nut biscuit, but so long as you include the lemon zest and use cane sugar molasses or black treacle, it will still have that inimitable flavour.

For the variation below, feel free to substitute other types of molasses as desired.

➳ For this craquelin, it is possible to replace the baking powder with a like measure of **sodium bicarbonate** (baking soda), which reacts with the molasses to create the leavening action.

or if you prefer...

1 T
1⅔ T

1 T
1 t

2¼ T
1⅔ T*

11 T
2 t
½ t
⅛ t
⅛ t

** packed*

◇ MOLASSES

- Omit the lemon zest
- For the spices, use

½ **t** of **ground cinnamon**
¼ **t** of **ground ginger**
a pinch of **ground cloves**

"Ginger nut"

20 g	**almond butter**	stir together in a bowl
25 g	**vegan milk**	
20 g	**molasses or black treacle**	add and mix well
2 g	**lemon zest** (≈ ¼ lemon)	
30 g	**blond cane sugar**	add and mix well
20 g	**rapadura sugar**	
80 g	**flour**	sift together, then add and mix well
2 t	**ground ginger**	
½ t	**baking powder**	
⅛ t	**sodium bicarbonate**	
⅛ t	**salt**	

Preheat the oven with the baking sheet to 180°C / 350°F / Gas mark 4.

Roll out the dough, directly onto a sheet of baking paper.

Optional: you can brush the dough with a bit of **vegan milk** or water and then add a light sprinkling of **blond cane sugar**.

If desired, cut the dough after 5 minutes of baking.

Bake for 6 minutes at 180°C, then reduce the thermostat to **120°C / 250°F / Gas mark ½** and continue baking with the oven door closed for 5 to 10 minutes. Then turn off the oven, open the door slightly and leave the craquelin inside, the time needed for it to become dry and crunchy as it cools completely.

or if you prefer...

These craquelins are inspired by the various *speculaas* cookies that are traditionally enjoyed during the end of year holidays in Northern Europe.

1 T
2 T

Along with pistachio, aniseed, sesame and cinnamon craquelins, these 'speculaas' make a lovely accompaniment to a cup tea or coffee...

2¼ T
2⅓ T *
½ t

The spice mixture

1 t	**ground cinnamon**	grind any spices that are whole, then mix all of the spices together
¼ t	**ground ginger**	
¼ t	**ground cloves**	
¼ t	**ground nutmeg**	
⅛ t	**allspice** (Jamaica pepper)	
⅛ t	**aniseed**	
1/16 t	**cardamom** (≈ 1 pod)	
pinch	**white pepper**	
pinch	**coriander**	

11 T
½ t
⅛ t

* *packed*

"Speculaas"

20 g	**almond butter**	stir together in a bowl
30 g	**vegan milk**	
30 g	**blond cane sugar**	add and mix well
30 g	**rapadura sugar**	
½ t	**vanilla sugar** or extract	
➳	**the spice mixture**	sift these ingredients together, then add and mix well
80 g	**flour**	
½ t	**baking powder**	
⅛ t	**salt**	

Preheat the oven with the baking sheet to 180°C / 350°F / Gas mark 4.

Roll out the dough, directly onto a sheet of baking paper.

Optional: you can brush the dough with a bit of **vegan milk** or water and then add a light sprinkling of **blond cane sugar** and/or **cinnamon**.

If desired, cut the dough after 5 minutes of baking.

Bake for 6 minutes at 180°C, then reduce the thermostat to **120°C / 250°F / Gas mark ½** and continue baking with the oven door closed for 5 to 10 minutes. Then turn off the oven, open the door slightly and leave the craquelin inside, the time needed for it to become dry and crunchy as it cools completely.

or if you prefer...

In 1938, in the kitchens of the Toll House Inn in Whitman, Massachusetts, Ruth Graves Wakefield and her co-chef Sue Brides baked the very first *Toll House Chocolate Crunch Cookie*. The cookies were an immediate hit, and Ruth happily began sharing her new recipe with anyone who asked. The four winds did the rest. Today, the 'chocolate chip' cookies that are baked the world over can all trace their origins back to Ruth's very first *Toll House* cookie.

➳ If you don't have chocolate chips, you can simply cut up a few squares of **dark chocolate** by hand – which is what Ruth and Sue were doing before the Nestlé company came up with the idea of supplying them with specially-made 'semi-sweet chocolate morsels'.

1 T

2 T

1¾ T

2 T*

½ t

11 T

½ t

⅛ t

1½ T

2 T (¾ oz)

** packed*

“Chocolate chip”

20 g	**almond butter** or hazelnut butter	stir together in a bowl
30 g	**vegan milk**	
25 g	**blond cane sugar**	add and mix well
25 g	**rapadura sugar**	
½ t	**vanilla sugar** or extract	
80 g	**flour**	sift together, then add and mix well
½ t	**baking powder**	
⅛ t	**salt**	
15 g	**hazelnuts**	chop the hazelnuts into small pieces, lightly toast them in a dry skillet, and **reserve**
20 g	**chocolate chips**	**reserve**

Preheat the oven with the baking sheet to 180 °C / 350 °F / Gas mark 4.

Roll out the dough, directly onto a sheet of baking paper.

Brush with **vegan milk** or water and then sprinkle with the **reserved hazelnuts**, using the rolling pin to lightly press them into the dough.

Bake for 6 minutes at 180 °C. Remove from the oven, proceed with cutting the dough if desired, then sprinkle with the **reserved chocolate chips**. Return the dough to the oven, reduce the thermostat to **120 °C / 250 °F / Gas mark ½** and continue baking with the oven door closed for 5 to 10 minutes. Then turn off the oven, open the door slightly and leave the craquelin inside, the time needed for it to become dry and crunchy as it cools completely.

or if you prefer...

The 'digestive biscuit' was first cooked up in Scotland as early as 1839. Its moniker derives from the fact that it is made with whole-grain flour and contains sodium bicarbonate, which are both known to aid digestion.

1 T
3⅓ T

1⅓ T
2 T*
½ t

→ This craquelin is also very satisfying when made twice as thick. Simply double the quantities and bake first for 8 minutes at 180°C, then as directed.

4 T
2 T

11 T
½ t
⅛ t
⅛ t

* packed

◇ **DIGESTIVE BISCUIT ~ CHIA** or **POPPY SEED**

- Add **10 g** (1 T) of **chia seeds** or **poppy seeds**

◇ **DIGESTIVE BISCUIT ~ DATES**

- Add **30 g** (3 T) of **dates**, cut into smaller pieces

◇ **DIGESTIVE BISCUIT ~ RAISINS**

- Add **30 g** (3 T) of **raisins** or **sultanas**, cut into smaller pieces

◇ **DIGESTIVE BISCUIT ~ SESAME**

- Add **10 g** (1 T) of either white or black **sesame seeds**, or a mix of both, lightly toasted in a dry pan beforehand

"Digestive biscuit"

20 g	**almond butter**	stir together in a bowl
50 g	**vegan milk**	
15 g	**blond cane sugar**	add and mix well
25 g	**rapadura sugar**	
½ t	**vanilla sugar** or extract	
25 g	**wheat germ**	add and mix well
5 g	**wheat bran**	
80 g	**wholewheat flour**	sift together, then add and mix well
½ t	**baking powder**	
⅛ t	**sodium bicarbonate**	
⅛ t	**salt**	

Preheat the oven with the baking sheet to 180 °C / 350 °F / Gas mark 4.

Roll out the dough, directly onto a sheet of baking paper.

Optional: you can brush the dough with a bit of **vegan milk** or water and then add a light sprinkling of **blond cane sugar**.

If desired, cut the dough after 5 minutes of baking.

Bake for 6 minutes at 180 °C, then reduce the thermostat to **120 °C / 250 °F / Gas mark ½** and continue baking with the oven door closed for 5 to 10 minutes. Then turn off the oven, open the door slightly and leave the craquelin inside, the time needed for it to become dry and crunchy as it cools completely.

or if you prefer...

1 T
2 T
3 T
½ t
11 T
½ t
⅛ t

To this simple sugar craquelin you can add any number of other ingredients – spices, dried fruits, seeds, nuts, herbs – or replace the blond cane sugar with a sugar of your choice, such as coconut sugar, date palm sugar, demerara, muscovado, turbinado, etc.

➻ For a colourful topping, proceed as follows: do not brush the dough with vegan milk, but do sprinkle it with a dark sugar such as muscovado. Next, cover with a sheet of baking paper to prevent sticking and use the rolling pin to press the sugar into the dough. Finally, remove the paper, and bake as directed.

➻ You can replace the flour with one or more other flours. If you use flours that are gluten-free, note that in terms of texture, the resulting craquelin will be more compact compared to those that are made with only wheat flour.

◇ BUCKWHEAT

- Replace the flour with **100 g** (14 T) of **buckwheat flour**

Dar tiempo al tiempo, que suele dar dulces salidas
a muchas amargas dificultades.

MIGUEL DE CERVANTES SAAVEDRA

Sugar ~ plain & simple

20 g	**almond butter**	stir together in a bowl
30 g	**vegan milk**	
40 g	**blond cane sugar**	add and mix well
½ t	**vanilla sugar** or extract	
80 g	**flour**	sift together, then add and mix well
½ t	**baking powder**	
⅛ t	**salt**	

Preheat the oven with the baking sheet to 180°C / 350°F / Gas mark 4.

Roll out the dough, directly onto a sheet of baking paper.

Optional: you can brush the dough with a bit of **vegan milk** or water and then add a light sprinkling of **blond cane sugar**. You can also sprinkle it with spices, such as **cinnamon** or **nutmeg**, and/or **cocoa**.

If desired, cut the dough after 5 minutes of baking.

Bake for 6 minutes at 180°C, then reduce the thermostat to **120°C / 250°F / Gas mark ½** and continue baking with the oven door closed for 5 to 10 minutes. Then turn off the oven, open the door slightly and leave the craquelin inside, the time needed for it to become dry and crunchy as it cools completely.

Whether they're made with lemon, lime or some other citrus fruit, these craquelins with their slightly tangy 'bite' are both delicious on their own, or served alongside a chilled dessert of your choice.

➳ You can make your own **concentrated lemon juice**. Once you have grated the lemon peel to obtain the zest, halve and squeeze the lemon to obtain the juice. Bring the juice to a boil in a small saucepan, then lower the heat and reduce the liquid by two-thirds.

Lemon icing

For a touch of added sweetness, brush the dough prior to baking with 1 T or more of **freshly squeezed lemon juice** and then add a light sprinkling of **blond cane sugar**.

◇ LEMON ~ DRIZZLED DARK CHOCOLATE ICING

- Brush the dough prior to baking with 1 T of **freshly squeezed lemon juice**; then, after 5 minutes of baking, add a **drizzled dark chocolate icing** per the instructions given on page 60

◇ LEMON ~ SESAME

- Add **10 g** (1 T) of either white or black **sesame seeds**, or a mix of both, lightly toasted in a dry skillet beforehand

or if you prefer...

1 T
1 T

1 T

2 T*
½ t

9½ T
4⅓ T*
½ t
⅛ t
⅛ t

1 T

** packed*

Lemon

20 g	**almond butter**	stir together in a bowl
5 g	**lemon zest** (≈ ½ lemon)	
15 g	**vegan milk**	add and mix well
15 g	**ground almonds**	add and mix well
½ t	**vanilla sugar** or extract	
70 g	**flour**	sift together, then add and mix well
50 g	**icing sugar**	
½ t	**baking powder**	
⅛ t	**sodium bicarbonate**	
⅛ t	**salt**	
15 g	**concentrated lemon juice**	add the juice last and mix well

Preheat the oven with the baking sheet to 180°C / 350°F / Gas mark 4.

Roll out the dough, directly onto a sheet of baking paper.

Optional: add a **lemon icing** (page opposite).

If desired, cut the dough after 5 minutes of baking.

Bake for 6 minutes at 180°C, then reduce the thermostat to **120°C / 250°F / Gas mark ½** and continue baking with the oven door closed for 5 to 10 minutes. Then turn off the oven, open the door slightly and leave the craquelin inside, the time needed for it to become dry and crunchy as it cools completely.

or if you prefer...

1 T
2 T

3 T
½ t

2 T

11 T
½ t
⅛ t

Native to the Levant, aniseed has been celebrated since antiquity for its culinary merits and medicinal virtues. Like sesame and poppy seeds, aniseed figures as a star ingredient in many pastries, both in Europe and throughout the Mediterranean.

◇ POPPY SEED

- Replace the aniseed by **30 g** (3 T) of **poppy seeds**

Aniseed

20 g	**almond butter**	stir together in a bowl
30 g	**vegan milk**	
40 g	**blond cane sugar**	add and mix well
½ t	**vanilla sugar** or extract	
15 g	**aniseed, whole**	add and mix well
80 g	**flour**	sift together, then add and mix well
½ t	**baking powder**	
⅛ t	**salt**	

Preheat the oven with the baking sheet to 180°C / 350°F / Gas mark 4.

Roll out the dough, directly onto a sheet of baking paper.

Optional: you can brush the dough with a bit of **vegan milk** or water and then add a light sprinkling of **blond cane sugar**.

If desired, cut the dough after 5 minutes of baking.

Bake for 6 minutes at 180°C, then reduce the thermostat to **120°C / 250°F / Gas mark ½** and continue baking with the oven door closed for 5 to 10 minutes. Then turn off the oven, open the door slightly and leave the craquelin inside, the time needed for it to become dry and crunchy as it cools completely.

In the Levant and Europe, the true origin of cinnamon remained a mystery for centuries. Coming from distant lands at great expense, it was hailed in ancient times as being a gift that befitted the greatest monarchs and even the gods.

Ceylon cinnamon – *Cinnamomum verum* or *zeylanicum*, considered to be the 'true' cinnamon – is the best in terms of aroma and taste. Its delicate flavour is however lost when heated. For this reason, it is *Cinnamomum cassia* – known as Chinese cinnamon, or cassia – that is to be preferred for baked goods, as its stronger, spicier flavour holds up well when heated. Even so, due to its significantly higher coumarin content, it should be consumed in moderation.

or if you prefer...

1 T
2 T

3 T
½ t

11 T
2 t
¼ t
½ t
⅛ t

◇ CINNAMON ~ CHOCOLATE CHIP

- Just prior to reducing the thermostat, sprinkle the half-baked dough with **20 g** (¾ oz or 2 T) of **chocolate chips**, or squares of dark chocolate that have been chopped into small pieces. (Alternatively, you can opt instead for a **drizzled dark chocolate icing**, p. 60.)

◇ GINGER

- For the spices, use

  2 t of **ground ginger**
  ¼ t of **ground cinnamon**
  optional: a small pinch of **ground cloves**

Cinnamon

20 g	**almond butter**	stir together in a bowl
30 g	**vegan milk**	
40 g	**blond cane sugar**	add and mix well
½ t	**vanilla sugar** or extract	
80 g	**flour**	sift together, then add and mix well
2 t	**ground cinnamon**	
¼ t	**ground ginger**	
½ t	**baking powder**	
⅛ t	**salt**	

Preheat the oven with the baking sheet to 180°C / 350°F / Gas mark 4.

Roll out the dough, directly onto a sheet of baking paper.

Optional: you can brush the dough with a bit of **vegan milk** or water and then add a light sprinkling of **blond cane sugar** and **ground cinnamon**.

If desired, cut the dough after 5 minutes of baking.

Bake for 6 minutes at 180°C, then reduce the thermostat to **120°C / 250°F / Gas mark ½** and continue baking with the oven door closed for 5 to 10 minutes. Then turn off the oven, open the door slightly and leave the craquelin inside, the time needed for it to become dry and crunchy as it cools completely.

or if you prefer...

→ You can make your own **concentrated orange juice**. Once you have grated the orange peel to obtain the zest, halve and squeeze the orange to obtain the juice – if you plan to add the icing, start with the juice of 2 oranges. Bring the juice to a boil in a small saucepan, then lower the heat and reduce the liquid by three-quarters.

1 T
1 to 2 T

2 t

For a slightly stronger orange flavour, you can replace the vegan milk with additional concentrated orange juice, or add 1 t **orange blossom water**.

½ t

11 T
4⅓ T*
½ t
⅛ t
⅛ t

Orange icing

For a touch of added sweetness, brush the dough prior to baking with 1 T or more of **concentrated orange juice** and then add a light sprinkling of **blond cane sugar**.

1 T

* *packed*

◆ ORANGE ~ DRIZZLED DARK CHOCOLATE ICING

- After 5 minutes of baking, add a **drizzled dark chocolate icing** per the instructions given on page 60

Orange

20 g	**almond butter**	stir together in a bowl
5 to 10 g	**orange zest** (≈ ½ to 1 orange)	
10 g	**vegan milk**	add and mix well
½ t	**vanilla sugar** or extract	add and mix well
80 g	**flour**	sift together, then add and mix well
50 g	**icing sugar**	
½ t	**baking powder**	
⅛ t	**sodium bicarbonate**	
⅛ t	**salt**	
15 g	**concentrated orange juice**	add the juice last and mix well

Preheat the oven with the baking sheet to 180 °C / 350 °F / Gas mark 4.

Roll out the dough, directly onto a sheet of baking paper.

Optional: you can brush the dough with a bit of **vegan milk** or water and then add a light sprinkling of **blond cane sugar** and/or **cinnamon**. Alternatively, you can add an **orange icing** (page opposite).

If desired, cut the dough after 5 minutes of baking.

Bake for 6 minutes at 180 °C, then reduce the thermostat to **120 °C / 250 °F / Gas mark ½** and continue baking with the oven door closed for 5 to 10 minutes. Then turn off the oven, open the door slightly and leave the craquelin inside, the time needed for it to become dry and crunchy as it cools completely.

or if you prefer...

3 T

1 T

1⅔ T

1 t

3 T

½ t

9½ T

⅛ t

½ t

⅛ t

Native to Central Asia and thriving in regions blessed with very cold winters and long, hot summers, pistachios have flourished in Iran since ancient times. No surprise then, that the pistachio occupies such an important place in Iranian cuisine… and especially its pastries, from which this craquelin takes its inspiration.

➳ If you plan to add the optional topping, be sure to toast an additional 15 g (2 T) of pistachios at the same time and **reserve**.

Note that pistachios with unopened hulls were not fully ripe when harvested; it is better to leave them aside.

Pistachio

20 g	**whole pistachios**, shelled	lightly toast the pistachios in a dry pan, then grind them to obtain a fine meal
20 g	**almond butter**	stir together in a bowl, and add the ground pistachios
25 g	**vegan milk**	
1 t	**rose water**	
40 g	**blond cane sugar**	add and mix well
½ t	**vanilla sugar** or extract	
70 g	**flour**	sift together, then add and mix well
⅛ t	**ground cardamom** (≈ 2 pods)	
½ t	**baking powder**	
⅛ t	**salt**	

Preheat the oven with the baking sheet to 180 °C / 350 °F / Gas mark 4.

Roll out the dough, directly onto a sheet of baking paper.

Optional: you can brush the dough with a bit of **vegan milk** or water and then add a sprinkling of **blond cane sugar** and/or chopped **pistachios** that have been lightly toasted, using the rolling pin to lightly press them into the dough.

If desired, cut the dough after 5 minutes of baking.

Bake for 6 minutes at 180 °C, then reduce the thermostat to **120 °C / 250 °F / Gas mark ½** and continue baking with the oven door closed for 5 to 10 minutes. Then turn off the oven, open the door slightly and leave the craquelin inside, the time needed for it to become dry and crunchy as it cools completely.

or if you prefer...

2½ T
2⅔ T

2¼ T
1⅔ T*
½ t

9½ T
½ t
¼ t

** packed*

Know by some as *monkey nuts* or *groundnuts*, peanuts are native to South America, where they have been cultivated for over a thousand years. Unlike walnuts, almonds or pistachios, the peanut does not grow on trees and is not a true nut. Rather, like chickpeas and lentils, it is the fruit of a leguminous plant... but this plant, *Arachis hypogaea*, is unlike any other, in that it develops its fruit underground.

◇ PEANUT BUTTER ~ CHOCOLATE CHIP

- Just prior to reducing the thermostat, sprinkle the half-baked dough with **20 g** (¾ oz or 2 T) of **chocolate chips**, or squares of dark chocolate that have been chopped into small pieces. (Alternatively, you can opt instead for a **drizzled dark chocolate icing**, p. 60.)

◇ CHOCOLATE ~ PEANUT BUTTER

- For the sugar, use **25 g** (1¾ T) of **blond cane sugar** and **15 g** (1⅓ T, packed) of **rapadura sugar**
- Add **15 g** (½ oz) of grated **dark chocolate**
- Replace the recipe's 70 g of flour with **50 g** (7¼ T) of **flour** and **15 g** (2 T) of **cocoa powder**, and roll out the dough using a mixture of flour and cocoa powder to prevent sticking (see p. 4)

Le contenu d'une cacahuète est suffisant
pour que deux amis puissent le partager.

BURKINABE PROVERB

Peanut butter

50 g	**peanut butter**	stir together in a bowl
40 g	**vegan milk**	
30 g	**blond cane sugar**	add and mix well
20 g	**rapadura sugar**	
½ t	**vanilla sugar** or extract	
70 g	**flour**	sift together, then add and mix well
½ t	**baking powder**	
¼ t	**salt**	

Preheat the oven with the baking sheet to 180 °C / 350 °F / Gas mark 4.

Roll out the dough, directly onto a sheet of baking paper.

Optional: you can sprinkle the dough with a few pinches of **sea salt**, fixing it in place with the rolling pin.

You can also brush the dough with a bit of **vegan milk** or water and then add a light sprinkling of **rapadura** or **blond cane sugar** (or a mixture of both) and/or 15 g (2 T) of chopped **peanuts**. Use the rolling pin to lightly press them into the dough.

If desired, cut the dough after 5 minutes of baking.

Bake for 6 minutes at 180 °C, then reduce the thermostat to **120 °C / 250 °F / Gas mark ½** and continue baking with the oven door closed for 5 to 10 minutes. Then turn off the oven, open the door slightly and leave the craquelin inside, the time needed for it to become dry and crunchy as it cools completely.

or if you prefer...

1 T
2 T

3 T
½ t

11 T
½ t
⅛ t

As you'll have probably noticed, there is no wasabi paste in the dough itself. Curiously, when wasabi is incorporated into the dough, its sharp flavour more or less disappears when baked... whereas when added in the form of an icing, it remains mysteriously present.

Were it possible, we would of course prefer to use a genuine wasabi root for making these craquelins. However, since wasabi roots are difficult to find outside of Japan, and in any case come at a prohibitive cost, the quantities given here are for the 'wasabi paste' that is commonly found in markets around the world.

Wasabi icing

For the icing, mix together

10 g (1½ t) of **wasabi paste**
15 g (1 T) of **vegan milk**
20 g (1⅔ T, packed) of **icing sugar**

Alternatively, you can brush the dough with a mixture of wasabi paste and vegan milk, and then simply sprinkle it with **blond cane sugar**.

Wasabi

20 g	**almond butter**	stir together in a bowl
30 g	**vegan milk**	
40 g	**blond cane sugar**	add and mix well
½ t	**vanilla sugar** or extract	
80 g	**flour**	sift together, then add and mix well
½ t	**baking powder**	
⅛ t	**salt**	
➛	**wasabi paste**	for the wasabi icing (page opposite)
	vegan milk	
	icing sugar	

Preheat the oven with the baking sheet to 180°C / 350°F / Gas mark 4.

Roll out the dough directly onto a sheet of baking paper.

Bake for 6 minutes at 180°C.

Remove the half-baked dough, slide the baking paper off the baking sheet onto your work surface, and apply the **wasabi icing.**

Proceed with cutting the dough if desired.

Return the half-baked craquelin to the oven and reduce the thermostat to **120°C / 250°F / Gas mark ½**. Continue baking with the oven door closed for 5 to 10 minutes, then turn off the oven, open the door slightly and leave the craquelin inside, the time needed for it to become dry and crunchy as it cools completely.

or if you prefer...

1 T
1⅔ T

1 T

3⅝ T
½ t

8 T
½ t
¼ t
½ t
⅛ t

For this recipe, you can use store-bought **candied ginger**, or you can make your own as follows:

Peel a large piece of **fresh ginger** and cut it into slices that are 3 to 5 mm thick (⅛" to ¼").

In a small saucepan, mix **250 g** (25 cl., 8½ fl. oz) of **water** with **250 g** (8¾ oz or 20 T) of **blond cane sugar**. Begin heating this on the stove, stirring to dissolve the sugar. When the sugar has dissolved, add the sliced ginger.

Bring to a boil; let the mixture boil 5 minutes; then, turn off the heat and let the mixture cool completely in the saucepan. Repeat this step – bring to a boil / boil 5 minutes / cool completely – five to six times in all, always insuring the mixture has cooled completely before starting again.

Remove the slices of ginger from the syrup and arrange them on a plate to dry. Afterwards, if you wish, you can dip the slices of candied ginger in blond cane sugar to keep them from sticking together when stored in an airtight container.

Bananas ripe and green, and ginger-root,
Cocoa in pods and alligator pears,
And tangerines and mangoes and grape fruit,
Fit for the highest prize at parish fairs

Claude McKay

Candied ginger

20 g	**almond butter**	stir together in a bowl
25 g	**vegan milk**	
10 g	**candied ginger**	finely cut the candied ginger into small pieces, then add and mix well
50 g	**blond cane sugar**	add and mix well
½ t	**vanilla sugar** or extract	
60 g	**flour**	sift together, then add and mix well
½ t	**ground ginger**	
¼ t	**ground cinnamon**	
½ t	**baking powder**	
⅛ t	**salt**	

Preheat the oven with the baking sheet to 180°C / 350°F / Gas mark 4.

Roll out the dough, directly onto a sheet of baking paper.

Optional: you can brush the dough with a bit of **vegan milk** or water and then add a light sprinkling of **blond cane sugar**.

If desired, cut the dough after 5 minutes of baking.

Bake for 6 minutes at 180°C, then reduce the thermostat to **120°C / 250°F / Gas mark ½** and continue baking with the oven door closed for 5 to 10 minutes. Then turn off the oven, open the door slightly and leave the craquelin inside, the time needed for it to become dry and crunchy as it cools completely.

or if you prefer...

Ah, sesame seeds… so magical! You surely know the story of Djuha? How 1 T
that friendly fool was duped into buying a sackful of seeds for ten times 2 T
the price? 'These aren't *sesame* seeds,' swore the swindling souk merchant.
'They're *camel* seeds. Sow them before sundown, Djuha, and you will see! 2 T
When the sun rises, your field will be full of camels.' And, lo and behold –
it was true! The sun rose, and what did Djuha see? His field full of camels!
Woken by his shouts of joy, a group of Bedouins, who'd arrived in the night
and unknowingly pitched their camp in Djuha's freshly sown field, came 3 T
rushing out of their tents. 'Oh! What's this?' they cried. 'Thief, you! You're ½ t
stealing our camels!' 'Not at all,' Djuha assured them. 'These camels are
mine, all mine. I planted the seeds, and just look how they've grown!'

11 T
½ t
⅛ t

Sesame

20 g	**almond butter**, or tahini	stir together in a bowl
30 g	**vegan milk**	
20 g	**sesame seeds** white, black, or both	lightly toast the sesame seeds in a dry skillet, then add and mix well
40 g	**blond cane sugar**	add and mix well
½ t	**vanilla sugar** or extract	
80 g	**flour**	sift together, then add and mix well
½ t	**baking powder**	
⅛ t	**salt**	

Preheat the oven with the baking sheet to 180°C / 350°F / Gas mark 4.

Roll out the dough, directly onto a sheet of baking paper.

Optional: you can brush the dough with a bit of **vegan milk** or water and then add a light sprinkling of **blond cane sugar** and/or **sesame seeds** that have been lightly toasted in a dry skillet.

If desired, cut the dough after 5 minutes of baking.

Bake for 6 minutes at 180°C, then reduce the thermostat to **120°C / 250°F / Gas mark ½** and continue baking with the oven door closed for 5 to 10 minutes. Then turn off the oven, open the door slightly and leave the craquelin inside, the time needed for it to become dry and crunchy as it cools completely.

or if you prefer...

1 T
2⅓ T

3 T
½ t

11 T
2 to 3 t
½ t
⅛ t

It was in China, towards the end of the first millennium, that rituals for the drinking of powdered green tea were first developed. Some two centuries later, the tea and the rituals traveled to the Land of the Rising Sun, where the 'tea ceremony' – to the point of becoming an art – was refined and elevated to its highest expressions...

Here, the powdered green tea that the Japanese call *matcha* gives these craquelins both a distinctive hue and a unique, herbaceous flavour, one that goes well with a freshly brewed cup of tea.

Matcha icing

~ **with granulated sugar**

Before baking, brush the rolled-out dough with a mixture of

1 to 2 t of **matcha** powdered green tea
15 g (1 T) of **vegan milk**

Then sprinkle with **blond cane sugar**.

~ **with icing sugar**

Just prior to reducing the thermostat, remove the half-baked craquelin and brush it with a mixture of

1 to 2 t of **matcha** powdered green tea
20 g (1⅓ T) of **vegan milk**
20 g (1⅔ T, packed) of **icing sugar**

Return it to the oven and continue baking as directed.

Matcha

20 g	**almond butter**	}	stir together in a bowl
35 g	**vegan milk**		
40 g	**blond cane sugar**	}	add and mix well
½ t	**vanilla sugar** or extract		
80 g	**flour**	}	sift together, then add and mix well
2 to 3 t	**matcha** powdered green tea		
½ t	**baking powder**		
⅛ t	**salt**		

Preheat the oven with the baking sheet to 180 °C / 350 °F / Gas mark 4.

Roll out the dough, directly onto a sheet of baking paper.

Optional: add a **matcha icing** (page opposite).

If desired, cut the dough after 5 minutes of baking.

Bake for 6 minutes at 180 °C, then reduce the thermostat to **120 °C / 250 °F / Gas mark ½** and continue baking with the oven door closed for 5 to 10 minutes. Then turn off the oven, open the door slightly and leave the craquelin inside, the time needed for it to become dry and crunchy as it cools completely.

or if you prefer...

1 T
1⅓ T

1½ T

3 T
½ t

11 T
½ t
⅛ t
⅛ t

Native to East Africa, the tamarind tree is today found in almost all tropical regions. The tangy flavour of the tree's fruit is a mainstay and much-appreciated ingredient in numerous dishes and drinks the world over. It is also an essential constituent of the now ubiquitous English sauce created in 1837 by Lea & Perrins.

Tamarind icing

~ with granulated sugar

Before baking, brush the rolled-out dough with a mixture of

1 to 2 t of **tamarind paste**
15 g (1 T) of **vegan milk**

Then sprinkle with **blond cane sugar**.

~ with icing sugar

Just prior to reducing the thermostat, remove the half-baked craquelin and brush it with a mixture of

20 g (1 T) of **tamarind paste**
20 g (1⅓ T) of **vegan milk**
45 g (3⅔ T, packed) of **icing sugar**

Return it to the oven and continue baking as directed.

◇ TAMARIND ~ CRANBERRY

- Add **30 g** (1 oz or 3 T) of **dried cranberries**, cut into smaller pieces

Tamarind

20 g	**almond butter**	stir together in a bowl
20 g	**vegan milk**	
30 g	**tamarind paste**	add and mix well
40 g	**blond cane sugar**	add and mix well
½ t	**vanilla sugar** or extract	
80 g	**flour**	sift together, then add and mix well
½ t	**baking powder**	
⅛ t	**sodium bicarbonate**	
⅛ t	**salt**	

Preheat the oven with the baking sheet to 180°C / 350°F / Gas mark 4.

Roll out the dough, directly onto a sheet of baking paper.

Optional: add a **tamarind icing** (page opposite).

If desired, cut the dough after 5 minutes of baking.

Bake for 6 minutes at 180°C, then reduce the thermostat to **120°C / 250°F / Gas mark ½** and continue baking with the oven door closed for 5 to 10 minutes. Then turn off the oven, open the door slightly and leave the craquelin inside, the time needed for it to become dry and crunchy as it cools completely.

Rose petals have long featured in Iranian cuisine. However, from the 10th century onwards, it was rose water – a by-product of the distillation of rose petals for perfume – that rose to prominence as an ingredient in the country's pastries and other dishes. The use of rose water subsequently spread to the Arab world and then to Europe, where it enjoyed great popularity... until it was superseded by an ingredient from the tropics that would take the world by storm in the 19th century: the vanilla bean.

◇ ORANGE BLOSSOM WATER

- Replace the rose water by an equal measure of **orange blossom water**

Having developed in a similar manner around the Mediterranean, orange blossom water has been used for cooking and baking since at least the 8th century. It is obtained from the flowers of the bitter, or Seville, orange tree.

or if you prefer...

1 T
1 T
2 t
3 T
½ t
11 T
½ t
⅛ t

Rose water

20 g	**almond butter**	}	stir together in a bowl
15 g	**vegan milk**		
10 g	**rose water**	}	add and mix well
40 g	**blond cane sugar**	}	add and mix well
½ t	**vanilla sugar** or extract		
80 g	**flour**	}	sift together, then add and mix well
½ t	**baking powder**		
⅛ t	**salt**		

Preheat the oven with the baking sheet to 180°C / 350°F / Gas mark 4.

Roll out the dough, directly onto a sheet of baking paper.

Optional: you can brush the dough quite simply with **2 t** of **rose water**.

Or, you can brush the dough with **2 t** of **rose water** and then add a light sprinkling of **blond cane sugar**.

If desired, cut the dough after 5 minutes of baking.

Bake for 6 minutes at 180°C, then reduce the thermostat to **120°C / 250°F / Gas mark ½** and continue baking with the oven door closed for 5 to 10 minutes. Then turn off the oven, open the door slightly and leave the craquelin inside, the time needed for it to become dry and crunchy as it cools completely.

or if you prefer...

1 T
2 T

1 T

3 T

11 T
½ t
⅛ t

Originally from the tropical forests of southern Mexico and Central America, vanilla is the fruit of an orchid that is today successfully cultivated around the world… all thanks to a discovery made on the Réunion island in 1841 by a young slave who would later be known as Edmond Albius.

Though only 12 years old at the time, it was the observant Edmond who was the first to imagine and develop a method, both economical and reliable, for pollinating the orchid's flowers by hand. It proved to be the missing piece of a puzzle that had long stumped the greatest naturalists of the time: in the orchid's native habitat, an indigenous bee insured the pollination – but the bee could not be exported with the same success as the orchid itself, and the naturalists had been hard pressed to find an effective workaround. Thanks to Albius' ingenuity, vanilla was made ripe to conquer the world…

➸ You can replace the vanilla sugar with liquid **vanilla extract**, but when doing so, reduce the quantity of vegan milk by 15 g (1 T).

◇ TONKA BEAN

- Replace the vanilla sugar with **2 tonka beans**, finely grated

The tonka bean is the seed of a tree that is native to South America. Although tonka's aroma resembles that of vanilla, it nevertheless has a unique and delicate flavour all its own. Note that the beans should be consumed with moderation, owing to their high coumarin content.

Vanilla

20 g	**almond butter**	}	stir together in a bowl
30 g	**vegan milk**		
1 T	**vanilla sugar**	}	add and mix well
40 g	**blond cane sugar**	}	add and mix well
80 g	**flour**	}	sift together, then add and mix well
½ t	**baking powder**		
⅛ t	**salt**		

Preheat the oven with the baking sheet to 180°C / 350°F / Gas mark 4.

Roll out the dough, directly onto a sheet of baking paper.

Optional: you can brush the dough with a bit of **vegan milk** or water and then add a light sprinkling of **blond cane sugar**, or a mixture of blond cane sugar and **vanilla sugar**.

If desired, cut the dough after 5 minutes of baking.

Bake for 6 minutes at 180°C, then reduce the thermostat to **120°C / 250°F / Gas mark ½** and continue baking with the oven door closed for 5 to 10 minutes. Then turn off the oven, open the door slightly and leave the craquelin inside, the time needed for it to become dry and crunchy as it cools completely.

"À bon port"

A word about...

Almond butter

You can replace almond butter – gram for gram – by another puree made from nuts or seeds, such as peanuts, chestnuts, hazelnuts, cashews, sesame (known as *tahini* or *tahin*), walnuts, etc.; or by a vegetable margarine; or, for non-vegans, by sweet cream butter.

Baking powder

By combining sodium bicarbonate and cream of tartar, you can make your own baking powder for immediate use. Replace ½ t of baking powder with a mixture of

- ¼ t cream of tartar
- ⅛ t sodium bicarbonate (baking soda)

Blond cane sugar

Relatively neutral in taste, blond cane sugar allows for sweetness to be added without unduly masking a craquelin's principle flavour. You can replace it with one or more other granulated sugars, with flavours that are more or less pronounced: coconut sugar, date palm sugar, demerara, turbinado...

Dark chocolate

In recipes that call for grated dark chocolate, use your favourite semi-sweet or bittersweet cooking chocolate containing at least 50% cocoa, or more as desired. Alternatively, you can substitute unsweetened baking chocolate, but you will likely want to increase the amount of sugar in the recipe.

Flour

The recipes in this book are in most cases made with plain, unbleached, all-purpose wheat flour in mind. The characteristics of the flour you use, or substituting a different flour, will necessarily affect the consistency of your dough; you can adjust for this by using more or less liquid. Gluten-free flours will give craquelins a texture that is somewhat more compact.

Malted yeast flakes

With a slightly sweet, nutty flavour, malted yeast flakes are a blend of malted barley and deactivated dried yeast. I personally prefer the taste of malted yeast flakes to the unmalted varieties of so-called nutritional yeast – which is also sometimes called *brewer's yeast*, as it is usually made from the *Saccharomyces cerevisiae* strain of yeast.

Milk – vegan or dairy

Most any vegan/plant-based milk – such as barley, buckwheat, hemp, millet, pea, potato, quinoa, soy, spelt, et cetera – can be used. For non-vegans, it can also be replaced gram for gram by dairy milk.

Olive oil

Olive oil can be replaced by another vegetable oil of your choice, so long as it is suitable for cooking – i.e. being subjected to heat – and has a flavour that you like.

Rapadura sugar

Coming from Latin America, rapadura or *panela* is an unrefined sugar that is notable for its marked flavour of molasses. It can be replaced by muscovado – an unrefined sugar from either Mauritius or the Philippines with an even more pronounced molasses flavour – or by one of the many other sorts of semi-refined or unrefined sugars, such as piloncillo, kokuto, or jaggery.

Sodium bicarbonate

Already known to the Egyptians in antiquity, sodium bicarbonate – also called *baking soda* – is a completely natural product. When combined with an acidic ingredient such as tomato sauce, molasses, tamarind, or orange or lemon juice, the reaction that follows tends to neutralize the acid; it also releases carbon dioxide, which produces a leavening action. When it is called for in a recipe, it insures that the craquelin's flavour will not be unduly acidic, and that its texture will be at its best.

Note too that better results are obtained whenever it is possible to add the acidic ingredient *after* the flour has been mixed in. This is why incorporating the concentrated orange and lemon juices, or the thick tomato sauce, is left to the final step when mixing the dough.

Tamari *(tamari-shōyu)*

The flavour of this traditional Japanese sauce is more nuanced and less salty than ordinary soy sauce; it also has a darker colour and is somewhat thicker. While both are made from fermented soybeans, the method of preparation for most soy sauces includes a certain amount of wheat. In contrast, tamari is a by-product of the production of soy-based miso, to which wheat is not usually added.

Worcestershire Sauce

This archetypal English sauce owes its distinctive taste to a key ingredient that confers a unique, tangy flavour: tamarind. For a vegan version, you can easily get along without the original recipe's anchovies... but you'll be hard pressed to make a good Worcestershire without tamarind!

Having acquainted myself with a number of different recipes, the following is one that I concocted for making the sauce and have enjoyed using:

vegan Worcestershire Sauce

		or if you prefer...
250 g	**cider vinegar**	17 T or 1 1/16 C
50 g	**water**	3 1/3 T or 1/4 C
100 g	**molasses** or **black treacle**	5 T
25 g	**tamarind paste**	3 T
75 g	**tamari**, or soy sauce	5 T or scant 1/3 C
40 g	**fresh lemon juice**	3 T
1	**small onion**, minced	
2	**garlic cloves**, crushed	
15 g	**blond cane sugar**	1 1/3 T
1 1/2 t	**salt**	
1 t	**ground ginger**	
1/2 t	**ground mustard seed**	
1/2 t	**ground black pepper**	
1/4 t	**ground cinnamon**	
1/4 t	**ground Cayenne pepper**	
1/8 t	**ground cloves**	
1/8 t	**ground cardamom**	≈ 2 pods

Prepare the onion and garlic. For the spices, use a mortar and pestle to grind those that are whole.

Put all of the ingredients into a large saucepan, cover, and bring to a gentle boil. Reduce the heat and simmer, covered, for about 30 minutes.

Using a stick blender or a food processor, puree the mixture. Let it cool, partially; then pour it through a strainer or sieve, and store in glass jars or bottles. Sterilize those you wish to save for later, and, once opened, keep the sauce in the refrigerator.

Nutritional information

The nutritional values that are presented here are to be read as informal guidelines. The calculated values can only be approximate, as there can be wide variations in the nutritional value of any given ingredient depending on where it was grown, the manner in which it was prepared and packaged, and the conditions under which it was subsequently stored.

The values are given **for one portion or serving**. In the main, there are 8 servings per recipe; but there are a few exceptions. Please check the table.

The nutritional values for the ingredients used in each recipe are based in most instances on those provided by the United States Department of Agriculture (USDA).

Since all of the recipes are vegan – even those that call for dark chocolate or chocolate chips, so long as they are dairy-free – the craquelins are cholesterol-free.

The list includes those variations that are preceded by a ◇ symbol in the book.

The calculations reflect the following important points:

- The nutritional values are based in first instance on the metric measure; if no metric measure is given, then according to the teaspoon or tablespoon measure. The values are based on the first ingredient or option, when several choices are given, and on the smallest measure when a range is proposed.
- The values for the sweet recipes are based on the use of unsweetened soy milk, unless otherwise specified (oat milk, coconut milk). Almond butter and peanut butter are considered to be pure, with no added salt or other ingredients.
- An additional 20 g of regular flour, or 10 g plus 10 g cocoa for chocolate recipes, is added to represent the flour that is worked into the dough when it is rolled out.
- The values do not take into account those ingredients measured as a 'pinch' or by 'drops', nor toppings or additions that are understood to be optional. As such – and especially for those who seek to regulate their intake of salt or sugar – please note that the addition of any optional sprinkling of salt or sugar, or the addition of an optional icing, will in any given recipe necessarily increase the values for either sodium or carbohydrates.

Savoury craquelins ~ nutritional values per serving

Recipe number	Page number	Craquelin	Servings per recipe	calories (kcal)	protein (g)	carbohydrates (g)	~ sugars (g)	total fat (g)	~ saturated (g)	~ monounsaturated (g)	~ polyunsaturated (g)	sodium (g)
10	29	**Chickpea**	8	79	2.7	9.7	1.0	3.2	0.5	1.9	0.5	0.10
	28	~ *chia* or *poppy seed*	8	86	2.9	10.0	1.0	3.7	0.5	2.0	0.9	0.10
	28	~ *garlic*	8	80	2.8	9.9	1.0	3.2	0.5	1.9	0.5	0.10
	28	~ *malted yeast*	8	79	3.4	8.9	1.3	3.1	0.4	1.8	0.5	0.10
	28	~ *sesame*	8	95	3.2	10.0	1.0	4.7	0.7	2.5	1.2	0.10
11	31	**Chili**	8	77	1.9	10.9	1.4	2.8	0.4	1.8	0.4	0.12
16	41	**Coconut ~ Curry**	8	98	2.1	11.7	1.6	4.8	2.7	1.5	0.3	0.11
3	15	**Cracked pepper**	8	80	2.5	11.0	0.4	2.8	0.4	1.8	0.3	0.10
	14	~ *garlic*	8	82	2.6	11.4	0.4	2.9	0.4	1.8	0.3	0.10
	14	~ *turmeric* or *curry*	8	82	2.6	11.2	0.4	2.9	0.4	1.8	0.3	0.10
12	33	**Curry ~ Sesame**	8	80	2.1	9.8	0.2	3.5	0.5	2.1	0.7	0.10
9	27	**Garlic ~ Sesame**	8	92	2.3	11.2	0.1	4.3	0.6	2.3	1.0	0.10
13	35	**Gomashio**	8	98	2.5	8.1	0.1	6.5	1.0	3.2	1.9	0.17
	34	~ *seaweed*	8	100	2.7	8.4	0.1	6.5	1.0	3.2	1.9	0.18
1	11	**Herbes de Provence**	8	79	2.1	11.2	0.2	2.7	0.4	1.8	0.3	0.10
	10	~ *black olive*	8	88	2.1	11.2	0.2	3.6	0.5	1.8	0.3	0.10
6	21	**Malted yeast**	8	77	3.5	9.1	0.9	2.7	0.4	1.7	0.3	0.10
	20	~ *chili pepper*	8	83	3.8	10.6	1.8	2.7	0.4	1.7	0.3	0.10
	24	*Poppy seed*	8	83	2.2	10.1	0.2	3.7	0.5	1.9	1.0	0.10
14	37	**Sambar**	8	99	2.6	10.4	0.2	5.3	0.7	3.0	1.3	0.10
7	23	**Savoury shortcrust**	12	125	3.6	12.7	0.6	6.8	1.0	3.3	2.0	0.13
15	39	**Seaweed**	8	85	2.2	9.8	0.1	4.3	0.7	2.3	1.0	0.07
	38	~ *with wasabi icing*	8	97	2.3	12.2	2.1	4.4	0.7	2.4	1.0	0.10
8	25	**Sesame**	8	86	2.3	9.7	0.2	4.2	0.6	2.3	1.0	0.10
	24	~ *smoked paprika*	8	91	2.5	10.6	0.3	4.5	0.7	2.4	1.1	0.10
4	17	**Tomato ~ Black olive**	8	87	2.2	11.1	0.7	3.6	0.5	1.8	0.3	0.15
2	13	**Wholewheat**	8	78	2.1	11.6	0.4	2.8	0.4	1.8	0.4	0.10
5	19	**Worcestershire**	8	79	2.7	10.4	0.7	2.7	0.4	1.7	0.3	0.18

Sweet craquelins ~ nutritional values per serving

Recipe number	Page number	Craquelin	Servings per recipe	calories (kcal)	protein (g)	carbohydrates (g)	– sugars (g)	total fat (g)	– saturated (g)	– monounsaturated (g)	– polyunsaturated (g)	sodium (g)
16	**75**	**Aniseed**	8	90	2,5	15,9	5,4	2,0	0,2	1,0	0,5	0,06
	70	*Buckwheat*	8	89	2.5	16.5	5.7	1.9	0.2	0.9	0.5	0.06
22	**87**	**Candied ginger**	8	84	1.8	15.5	7.6	1.6	0.1	0.8	0.5	0.06
6	**55**	**Chocolate**	8	93	2.7	14.7	6.5	3.6	0.8	1.8	0.7	0.06
	52	*~ coconut*	8	106	2.2	15.8	7.7	4.7	2.7	1.2	0.4	0.07
	54	*~ Espelette pepper*	8	93	2.7	14.7	6.5	3.6	0.8	1.8	0.7	0.06
	58	*~ lemon*	8	94	2.6	15.1	6.6	3.6	0.8	1.8	0.7	0.08
	82	*~ peanut butter*	8	104	3.3	15.1	6.5	4.4	1.1	2.0	0.8	0.12
	54	*~ quinoa*	8	97	2.9	15.4	6.4	3.7	0.8	1.8	0.8	0.06
9	**61**	**Chocolate ~ Intensely so**	8	96	2.9	14.8	6.2	3.8	1.0	1.8	0.7	0.06
	60	*~ drizzled dark chocolate icing*	10	98	2.5	14.3	6.9	4.4	1.5	1.9	0.6	0.05
7	**57**	**Chocolate ~ Mint**	8	93	2.7	14.7	6.5	3.6	0.8	1.8	0.7	0.06
	56	*~ drizzled mint chocolate icing*	10	96	2.3	14.1	7.1	4.2	1.4	1.9	0.6	0.05
8	**59**	**Chocolate ~ Orange**	8	101	2.8	16.5	7.1	3.6	0.8	1.8	0.7	0.08
	58	*~ drizzled dark chocolate icing*	10	102	2.4	15.6	7.6	4.2	1.4	1.8	0.6	0.07
12	**67**	**“Chocolate chip”**	8	113	2.6	17.9	7.9	3.6	0.7	2.0	0.6	0.06
17	**77**	**Cinnamon**	8	85	2.2	15.5	5.4	1.7	0.1	0.8	0.5	0.06
	76	*~ chocolate chip*	8	98	2.3	17.0	6.7	2.5	0.6	1.1	0.5	0.06
5	**53**	**Coconut**	8	98	1.9	15.0	6.7	3.6	2.0	0.9	0.4	0.07
	52	*~ drizzled dark chocolate icing*	10	100	1.7	14.4	7.3	4.2	2.4	1.2	0.4	0.06
	52	*~ orange*	8	98	2.0	15.8	7.3	3.2	1.6	0.9	0.4	0.07
2	**47**	**Coffee**	8	89	2.2	15.6	5.7	2.0	0.2	0.8	0.4	0.07
	46	*~ café au chocolat*	10	89	1.8	14.5	6.4	2.7	0.9	1.1	0.4	0.05
13	**69**	**“Digestive biscuit”**	8	94	3.0	17.1	5.7	2.1	0.2	0.9	0.8	0.08
	68	*~ chia* or *poppy seed*	8	101	3.2	17.4	5.7	2.6	0.3	1.0	1.1	0.09
	68	*~ dates*	8	104	3.1	19.9	8.1	2.1	0.2	0.9	0.8	0.08
	68	*~ raisins*	8	105	3.1	20.0	8.1	2.1	0.2	0.9	0.8	0.09
	68	*~ sesame*	8	102	3.3	17.2	5.7	2.9	0.3	1.2	1.1	0.09
	76	*Ginger*	8	85	2.2	15.3	5.4	1.7	0.2	0.8	0.5	0.06
10	**63**	**“Ginger nut”**	8	95	2.2	18.1	8.2	1.7	0.2	0.8	0.5	0.08
1	**45**	**Hazelnut**	8	105	2.6	13.9	5.6	4.7	0.4	3.1	0.9	0.06
15	**73**	**Lemon**	8	95	2.4	16.1	6.8	2.6	0.2	1.4	0.7	0.08
	72	*~ drizzled dark chocolate icing*	10	97	2.1	15.4	7.4	3.4	1.0	1.6	0.6	0.07

Recipe number	Page number	Craquelin	Servings per recipe	calories (kcal)	protein (g)	carbohydrates (g)	– sugars (g)	total fat (g)	– saturated (g)	– monounsaturated (g)	– polyunsaturated (g)	sodium (g)
	73	*~ sesame*	8	103	2.6	16.3	6.8	3.3	0.3	1.7	1.0	0.08
24	**91**	**Matcha**	8	85	2.3	15.2	5.4	1.7	0.2	0.9	0.5	0.06
	62	*Molasses*	8	94	2.1	17.9	8.2	1.7	0.1	0.8	0.5	0.08
18	**79**	**Orange**	8	90	2.1	17.1	7.2	1.6	0.1	0.8	0.4	0.08
	78	*~ drizzled dark chocolate icing*	10	94	1.9	16.1	7.7	2.6	0.9	1.1	0.4	0.07
	94	*Orange blossom water*	8	82	2.1	14.9	5.4	1.6	0.1	0.8	0.5	0.06
20	**83**	**Peanut butter**	8	105	3.1	16.1	6.8	3.4	0.5	1.7	0.8	0.12
	82	*~ chocolate chip*	8	118	3.2	17.6	8.0	4.2	1.0	1.9	0.8	0.12
	44	*Pecan*	8	109	2.3	13.8	5.6	5.2	0.5	2.9	1.5	0.06
	44	*Pine nut*	8	108	2.6	13.8	5.6	5.1	0.4	1.8	2.2	0.06
19	**81**	**Pistachio**	8	93	2.5	14.7	5.6	2.8	0.3	1.5	0.8	0.06
	74	*Poppy seed*	8	103	2.9	16.0	5.5	3.2	0.3	1.1	1.6	0.06
3	**49**	**Rolled oats**	12	113	3.3	17.6	6.2	3.6	0.4	1.3	1.4	0.06
26	**95**	**Rose water**	8	82	2.1	14.9	5.4	1.6	0.1	0.8	0.5	0.06
23	**89**	**Sesame**	8	99	2.7	15.2	5.4	3.2	0.4	1.4	1.1	0.06
4	**51**	**Shortbread**	12	144	3.8	19.9	7.5	5.8	0.7	2.4	2.2	0.08
11	**65**	**"Speculaas"**	8	94	2.2	17.8	7.9	1.7	0.2	0.8	0.5	0.06
14	**71**	**Sugar ~ plain & simple**	8	83	2.2	14.9	5.4	1.7	0.1	0.8	0.5	0.06
25	**93**	**Tamarind**	8	87	2.2	15.8	5.8	1.7	0.1	0.8	0.5	0.08
	92	*~ cranberry*	8	98	2.2	18.9	8.5	1.7	0.1	0.9	0.5	0.08
	96	*Tonka bean*	8	85	2.2	14.9	5.3	1.9	0.3	0.8	0.5	0.06
27	**97**	**Vanilla**	8	89	2.2	16.4	6.8	1.7	0.1	0.8	0.5	0.06
	44	*Walnut*	8	107	2.6	13.8	5.5	4.9	0.4	1.3	2.8	0.06
21	**85**	**Wasabi**	8	97	2.2	17.9	8.0	1.8	0.2	0.9	0.5	0.10

Index

Allspice, 64
Almond butter, **100**
Almond, bitter, 54
Almonds, 23, 37, 48, 51, 55, 57, 59, 61, 73
Aniseed, 64, 75
Apricots, 48

Baking powder, **100**
Baking sheet, size, 4, 7
Baking, time, 6
Buckwheat flour, 70

Cardamom, 64, 81, 103
Cashew nuts, 23, 51
Cayenne pepper, 103
Chia seeds, 28, 48, 68
Chickpea, flour, 29
Chili powder, 31
Chili pepper, 20
Chocolate chips, 52, 54, **66**, 67, 76, 82
Chocolate, dark, 52, 54, 55, 56, 57, 59, 60, 61, 66, 82, **100**
Chocolate icing, drizzled, 46, 52, 54, 58, **60**, 72, 76, 78, 82
Cinnamon, 62, 64, 76, 77, 87, 103
Cloves, 62, 64, 76, 103
Cocoa powder, 2, 4, 46, 52, 55, 57, 59, 61, 82
Coconut milk, 41, 52, 53
Coconut, shredded, 41, 52, 53
Coffee, 47, 54
Coriander, 64
Cranberries, 48, 92
Cream of tartar, **100**
Curcuma, 14
Curry powder, 14, 33, 41

Dates, 48, 68
Dough, golden rules, 2
Dough, how to cut, 5-6
Dough, how to roll out, 4

Espelette pepper, 54

Figs, 48
Flaxseeds, 37, 48
Flour, **101**
Flour, whole wheat, 13, 69

Garlic, 14, 27, 103
Garlic, granulated or powder, 28
Ginger, 62, 63, 64, 76, 77, 87, 103
Ginger, candied, **86**, 87
Gomashio, 35

Hazelnut butter, 45, 67
Hazelnuts, 23, 45, 48, 51, 67
Herbes de Provence, 11, 17

Icing, when to add, 4

Jamaica pepper, 64

Lemon juice, 58, 72, 103
Lemon juice, concentrated, 58, **72**, 73
Lemon zest, 58, 63, 73
Linseeds, 37, 48

Mango, 48
Matcha green tea, 54, 90, 91
Measuring the ingredients, 3
Milk – vegan or dairy, **101**
Mint chocolate drizzled icing, **56**
Molasses, 62, 63, 103
Mustard seed, ground, 103

Nutmeg, 64
Nutritional information, 104-107

Index

Oat milk, 47
Oats, rolled, 49
Olive oil, **101**
Olives, black, Greek-style, 10, 17
Onion, 10, 103
Orange blossom water, 58, 78, 94
Orange juice, concentrated, 52, **58**, 59, **78**, 79
Orange zest, 52, 59, 79

Paprika, 24
Paprika, smoked, 24
Peanut butter, 83
Peanuts, 83
Pecans, 44, 48
Pepper, 15, 103
Pepper, Cayenne, 103
Pepper, Espelette, 54
Pepper, white, 64
Peppermint oil, **56**, 57
Peppers, fresh, 20
Pie crust, 7
Pine nuts, 44
Pineapple, 48
Pistachios, 80, 81
Poppy seeds, 24, 28, 74
Prunes, 48
Pumpkin seeds, 49

Quinoa, 48, 54

Raisins, 49, 68
Rapadura, **101**
Raspberries, 48
Rose water, 81, 95

Sambar powder, 37
Sea salt, 35
Seaweed, 34, 38, 39
Sesame seed oil, 25
Sesame seeds, 23, 25, 27, 28, 33, 35, 39, 37, 48, 51, 68, 72, 89
Sodium bicarbonate, 17, 19, 62, 63, 69, 73, 79, 93, 100, **102**
Soy sauce, 19, **102**, 103
Store, best way to, 7
Sugar, blond cane, **100**
Sugar, icing, 38, 46, 73, 79, 84, 85, 90, 92
Sugar, rapadura, **101**
Sugar, vanilla, 97
Sultanas, 49, 68
Sunflower seeds, 49

Tahini, 89, 100
Tamari sauce, 19, **102**, 103
Tamarind paste, 92, 93, 103
Tea, matcha, 54, 90, 91
Temperature for baking, 6
Time, baking, 6
Topping, when to add, 4
Tomato sauce, thick, **16**, 17
Tonka bean, 96
Turmeric, 14

Utensils, kitchen, 3

Vinegar, cider, 103

Walnuts, 23, 44, 48, 51
Wasabi paste, 38, 54, 84, 85
Wheat bran, 69
Wheat germ, 69
Worcestershire sauce, 19, **102**
Worcestershire sauce, vegan recipe, 103

Yeast flakes, malted, **20**, **101**

About the author

A native of California, Peter Gillies traveled widely before putting down roots on an island off the French coast. He is a writer of seriocomic fiction, children's stories and freewheeling exegeses, a singer-songwriting acoustic guitarist, and an art and photography and cinema aficionado. He is also a devoted baker who does his level best to keep his children well supplied with manna from his oven...

About the illustrator

Magdalena Adomeit began her life in Germany with a pencil in hand and has been drawing ever since. Having studied illustration at the University of Applied Sciences (HAW) in Hamburg, with a special focus on children's books, she is today a traveling freelance illustrator for book and editorial illustration. You can learn about her art projects and ongoing travels at magdalenaadomeit.com and follow her on Instagram @magdalenaadomeit

Acknowledgements

It is clearly thanks to the contributions and encouragements of many people that this book has been able to arrive, as we say in French, *à bon port*.

A core crew of faithful taste-testers were always on hand to render a verdict vis-à-vis my latest explorations: without the stalwart support of Francine, Yo, Sophie, Frank and Gérard (to whom I am indebted for having proposed the French word *craquelin* as an apt moniker), I would have surely gone astray. Their preferences and ideas helped chart my course throughout this journey.

En route, other friends and well-wishers likewise chipped in with feedback and suggestions. I thank Alain, Aline, Anne-Marie, Camille, Charlotte, Dominique, the team at the *Eldorado*, Emilie, Eric, Françoise, Katerina, Kyoko, Luisa, Marie, Monique, Noga, Pascal, Sara, Valérie, and Zoé – with extra special thanks going to Valentina and to my children, Margot, Nathan, Gabriel, and Hannah, for their many contributions.

Christine, Cécile and Eric at the *Jardin de la Josière* cultivated the cereals and milled the flours that I used. What joy to work with good ingredients, locally produced and organic to boot!

Alain Dhouailly, a bookseller in Paris who specialises in rare books, tracked down the poet whose verses appear in the epigraph.

My nephew Andrew was happy to oblige when queried about bosons and early drafts. Most especially, my kitchen-savvy sister Barbara weighed in with scores of constructive remarks, putting to rights more than one oversight.

Maggie arrived *au bon moment* to see the odyssey through to its final port of call, bringing these pages to life with her creative imagination and artwork.

Shanghaied for a final reread (though possibly enticed by double-rations of craquelins), Yo Claux insured everything was shipshape before we docked.

Finally, a special note of thanks to Francine Fèvre. With an unflagging attention to detail, she edited and corrected my original French manuscript, aided me as I made innumerable revisions, and was always quick to give a frank opinion that would invariably lead to yet another amelioration. From the start, this book was able to steer clear of many a shoal, thanks to her precious guidance.

My gratitude to all... *merci et gracias à toutes y a todas, et à tous y a todos.*

Quotations

PAGE v Amédée Pommier, Océanides et fantaisies, *A mon frère*
PAGE 20 Clive Barker, *Abarat*
PAGE 30 Julos Beaucarne, *Ton Christ est juif*
PAGE 34 Renée Vivien, Cendres et Poussières, *Sonnet*
PAGE 38 19th century, author unknown, variously attributed
PAGE 48 Jeppe Aakjær, Vejr og Vind og Folkesind, *Havren*
PAGE 70 Miguel de Cervantes Saavedra, *La gitanilla*
PAGE 86 Claude McKay, Harlem Shadows, *The Tropics in New York*

Typographical note

Texts set in Angie Sans
➳ vignette set in Ambroise
Title, motto and ◆ set in Anisette
vignettes set in Le Monde Livre Classic
vignette set in Apolline

} Jean-François Porchez
typofonderie.com

Quotations and colophon texts
set in DTL Haarlemmer

} Jan van Krimpen /
Frank E. Blokland
dutchtypelibrary.nl

A·B·C· EDITIONS
17840 • LA BRÉE • FRANCE
ABCEDITIONS.COM

PRINTED IN THE UNITED STATES,
GREAT BRITAIN, AND IN OTHER COUNTRIES

CRAQUELINS • ENGLISH EDITION
 • ISBN 978-2-9570286-3-4

RETAIL PRICE IN FRANCE WHEN PUBLISHED • €24
DÉPÔT LÉGAL • APRIL 2022

artists•bistro•café•

www.ingramcontent.com/pod-product-compliance
Ingram Content Group UK Ltd.
Pitfield, Milton Keynes, MK11 3LW, UK
UKHW060119010826
14089UKWH00005B/65